When Fact Is Fiction

Documentary Art in the Post-Truth Era

Nele Wynants (ed.)

Antennae-Arts in Society
Valiz, Amsterdam

When Fact Is Fiction

Documentary Art in the Post-Truth Era

Nele Wynants (ed.)

Contributors

Pascal Gielen
Andrea Gorki
Charlotte Lybeer
Sigrid Merx
Patrícia Portela
Jonas Rutgeerts
Nienke Scholts
Katharina Smets
Elly Van Eeghem
Peter Van Goethem
Stefan Vanthuyne
Ludovik Vermeersch
Nele Wynants

Contents

Documentary Art in the Post-Truth Era
An Introduction

Nele Wynants

In 2016, 'post-truth' was selected as the word of the year by the Oxford English Dictionary. This had everything to do with the British referendum on EU membership and the American presidential elections, both events in which objective facts proved less important than emotion-driven public opinion. Analysts claim that we are living in a 'post-truth era' in which facts, the truth, and reality are increasingly undermined, while fiction is given a status upgrade. Though journalists do their utmost to uphold the high standards of objectivity that come with their profession by distinguishing fake news from carefully researched information, the social media are teeming with alternative facts, often spread by big data companies. The relationship between fact and fiction, truth and lie, has become an increasingly tense one.

Fiction is the domain of the writer and the artist, not of the journalist or the politician. Not that fiction has nothing to do with truth and reality. Quite the contrary. 'A writer lies the truth', Dutch author Simon Carmiggelt wrote. We know that a story arranges facts into a narrative, sometimes embellishing and reshuffling them. Fiction is honest in that it doesn't claim to be telling the truth. But even if fiction belongs to the imaginative realm, that doesn't mean that stories are inherently untrue. Perhaps stories reveal a deeper truth about the world in which we live than statistics or measurable facts. Fiction can open up the world, clarify it, but also question it. Or offer a different perspective. In addition, fiction hints at a wide range of possibilities. It allows us think up and imagine other realities, explore new perspectives on the future, or represent something that is hard or even impossible to represent otherwise. Thus, fiction pulls us into the world of the possible, the thinkable, the speculative, which–not coincidentally–also help some sciences in formulating hypotheses and assumptions, thinking out of the box and exploring new territories.

'The theory of fiction is perhaps the most difficult aspect of the philosophy of literature.' This is the captivating opening line of Terry Eagleton's chapter 'The Nature of Fiction' in his book *The Advent of Literature*.[1] The term 'fiction' indeed draws us into the semantic field of literary theory and philosophy, yet it doesn't have to end there. Theatre, film, photography, as well as the visual arts and audio performances use fiction too, as the chapters of this book make abundantly clear. Yet the most profound theoretical interest in fiction–as well as 'its fair share of embarrassing banalities', according to Eagleton—can be found in literary studies, though we should be careful not to treat literature and fiction as synonyms. To quote Bennison Gray's concise yet problematic definition: 'a fiction is a statement that refers to a made-up event, an event that has been invented or feigned rather than having actually happened'.[2] This description is useful to us because it immediately clarifies the stakes of this book: contrary to what Gray suggests, the distinction between fact and fiction is anything but a stable, dual relationship, and throughout history the line between the two has often been blurred. Take Cicero, who thought the historian also had to be an artist, or Quintilian, who regarded historiography as a form of 'poetry in prose'. Myths, legends and political justifications were part and parcel of early historiography, which rarely limited itself to listing the facts.[3]

In short, the relationship between fact and fiction is complex but inevitable. This observation does not even depend on authorial intention. After all, the 'fictionalizing reading' of a work of nonfiction can exceed the author's intentions. Yet the reverse is also true: readers can take a writer's fiction for reality. An eighteenth-century bishop who tossed *Gulliver's Travels* into the flames, exclaiming he didn't believe a word of it, comes to mind.[4] Or a statement can be false now, but become true later on. Think of *1984*, Orwell's dystopian science fiction novel from 1948 set in the future, which is nowadays regarded as a visionary book that became eerily recognizable. It works the other way around as well. Over time, the status of a work can shift from fictional to nonfictional. This is exactly how the Bible was interpreted by Western intellectual atheists: no longer as history, but as fiction. All of this goes to show that the so-called truth value is hardly a valid criterion to distinguish fact from fiction.

Today, some authors share the opinion that 'fictional propositions are neither true nor false because they are not meant to be genuine assertions in the first place', Eagleton argues.[5] But this statement too should be nuanced. After all, works of fiction often present us with specific and clear suggestions. Sometimes they build a view of reality that does more to help us gain insight into the world we live in than, say, a scientific analysis or a journalistic piece. The power of a text, an image, or a work of art may lie precisely in its presentation of a worldview that closely corresponds to our experience of reality, even though we know full well that its empirical basis is dubious or fictional. The reader's or viewer's double consciousness is an inherent quality of the aesthetic experience. We can be deeply moved by something we know to be 'just' fiction. What's more, the framework of fiction allows us to immerse ourselves in a piece of fiction without losing our ability to critically assess the world it evokes.[6]

Many theories on literature and fiction therefore put the reader's faith centre stage—a principle that is also known as the 'willing suspension of disbelief'. This phrase was coined by the English poet Samuel T. Coleridge. The poetry collection *Lyrical Ballads* (1817) contains both poems by Coleridge and his friend William Wordsworth and essays on the nature of poetry. According to Coleridge, writing or reading poetry requires 'that willing suspension of disbelief for the moment, which constitutes poetic faith'.[7] This famous quote expresses the fascinating idea that readers should accept the poem on their own terms and suspend their disbelief in fiction for the duration of the story in order to surrender to the premise of the fictional world. Ever since, the expression has been used to describe the ability to assimilate—the prerequisite for any emotional involvement in a fictional situation, notably drama or the fiction of film or literature. It once again points to a kind of double consciousness that characterizes our reading and viewing experience.

In addition, something may well be both fact and fiction at the same time. 'Fact can be fiction and fiction fact', philosopher of art Kendall Walton wrote in his magnum opus *Mimesis as Make-Believe: On the Foundations of the Representational Arts*.[8] Walton's 'make-believe theory' is centred on the idea that the term 'fictional' can mean 'true in the appropriate game of make-believe' or in the fictional world of representation.[9] According to Walton, the representational arts can be considered 'props' that stimulate specific imaginations, in the way that kids' toys (like dolls and teddy bears) serve as props in the fantasy world of children. Following the same logic, art evokes fictional truths. Fact and fiction coincide in this game of make-believe, meaning that a fictional story can be composed entirely of empirical truths.

When translated to the world of theatre this becomes even easier to imagine. Documentary theatre often relies on empirical sources, transposing them to the theatrical universe, the world of representation.[10] Yet, as Carol Martin rightly (and bluntly) puts it in her book *Theatre of the Real* (2013), the truth claims of many documentary theatre makers are naïve and beside the point.

The essence of what she refers to as the 'theatre of the real' has little to do with veracity, but lies in the way this veracity itself is problematized. The aim of documentary theatre, to continue quoting Martin, is not to reveal the truth, but to cause 'ontological theatre doubt' by deliberately blurring the distinction between reality and fiction, just like the distinction is vague in our daily reality, where our contact with the 'real' is always mediated.[11] Theatre does not stage reality, but makes the audience aware of this mediation, of the essentially theatrical nature of reality. At the same time, the actors on stage–their bodies, their voices and presence–are more real than any work of art. After all, audience and actors share the same space and time.[12] Theatre, then, seems to be the place where fact and fiction have always already shared the stage, performing their complex interplay.

This book brings together contributions by and about artists that probe the boundaries between fact and fiction. The ambiguous relationship between the documentary and the imagination is the common thread. The artists in question often draw on historical sources, oral testimonies, and archive material, translating their empirical sources into an artistic universe and deliberately blurring the boundaries between what is generally known as 'fiction' and as 'reality'. Indeed, they share a fascination with the same 'problem': the impossible challenge of representing reality. This 'problem' branches off into a number of related questions. What might be the role of fiction at a time when fake news, alternative facts, and infotainment undermine the integrity of politics and the media? What is the place of the imagination in how we understand and create the reality around us? What is the notion of truth that underlies this work?

The first part, *Reinventions of the Archive*, consists of texts by and about artists working with archive material. These artists examine the relation between the factual and the artistic representation of history by delving into historical sources. Their archive-based work corresponds to what art critic Hal Foster refers to as an 'archiving impulse' in contemporary art, with artists 'seek[ing] to make historical information, often lost or displaced, physically present'.[13] These artists indeed share an interest in historical research, albeit not with the aim of reconstructing or representing history. In most cases, the archival sources are evoked in 'a gesture of alternative knowledge or counter-memory'.[14] By purposely exploring the boundary between fact and fiction they reveal a different perspective on the past. Their artistic approach to archival sources enables them to develop new interpretations of history.

In this kind of work, the archival document is 'a critical form', to quote Sophie Berrebi.[15] By this the art historian means that it facilitates a critical analysis of issues such as representation, knowledge production, art, and history. Using the document as a critical form in their work, the artists thematize issues at play in our culture at large, such as the tense relationship between the museum and the archive, the confidence instilled in documents today, the way visual documents circulate in the art world and beyond. They connect actual events to historical events and reveal how the past reverberates in the present. At the same time, they reflect on the medium they use, and hence on how information is generated and shared these days.

The first chapter discusses several projects by young theatre makers working with historical sources without, however, creating documentary theatre in the strict sense of the word. Thomas Bellinck, Elly Van Eeghem, and Chokri and Zouzou Ben Chikha place their artistic projects and the sources they use in a fictional frame, thus trying to relate to a changing historical, social, or political reality. By stepping squarely into this reality and engaging in a dialogue with it, these artists deliberately blur the line between fact and fiction. They do not pursue an objective truth, nor a historically accurate representation of the past, yet they do encourage alternative imaginings of the reality in which these things take place. Thus they offer alternative perspectives on European history, urban development in a globalizing world, and the way we come to terms with our colonial past.

The archive is the protagonist in Peter Van Goethem's contribution as well. In *Brussel gefilmde stad* [Brussels captured on film], which appeared on DVD, the author compiled an inventory of how Brussels is portrayed in movie history. Using a selection of archive films from the Brussels Cinematek's movie collection, he subsequently created a found-footage science fiction film. The film fictionalizes its historical sources and simultaneously reflects on (cultural) memory and the archive. Van Goethem's contribution raises the question of whether there is such a thing as 'the memory of the city' and, if so, how fiction can offer new perspectives on representations of the past.

Patrícia Portela, too, uses both existing and self-created archival sources to rewrite the life of the historical character Acácio Nobre (1869–1968), a homo universalis who made his mark in Portuguese avant-garde circles. Using Nobre's unfinished projects and sketches of ideas as a starting point, she launched several artistic projects, such as an audio installation at the National Museum of Contemporary Art in Lisbon (MNAC), a concert performance that toured Europe, and a book dedicated to a part of his heritage. Composing Nobre's archive, Portela revives the collective memory of a nation, as well as offering an idiosyncratic perspective on Portuguese history at the beginning of the previous century.

The second series of contributions, *Alternative Visions on the Present*, zooms in on the artist's subjective perception and their views on contemporary reality. After all, an artist's view is always subjective—this, of course, being their privileged position, contrary to that of a hard scientist who strives for objectivity and measurability. We should obviously also acknowledge the subjective position in some 'softer' social sciences and the humanities. Feminist studies, ethnography and narrative studies, for instance, helped make us see that human subjectivity is indeed inevitable in science, and that not everything about the universe and our position in it can be understood based on measurements.[16] In the wake of deconstructivist theory, historiographers, too, realized that writing history is a narrative act undertaken by the historian in the present.[17] Yet it goes without saying that artists have privileged access to the toolbox of fiction. Precisely because they are explicit about their subjective position, they may be more trustworthy than journalists or historians. Using the framework of fiction, they open up new perspectives on the world, the city, the neighbourhood in which they live.[18]

Radio producer Katharina Smets, for instance, stages herself in her documentary podcasts, which offer a subjective view (or rather: sound) of the reality in which she installs her audio recorder. She evolved from documentary radio producer to autobiographical narrator, thus becoming an active character in her own audio stories. This entailed a different set of rules for structuring the reality she wanted to (re-)present. Smets explains how the I-narrator's emancipation proved a powerful concept for making audio stories. Thus, she reminds us that there's not one, but many subjective truths existing side by side.

Stefan Vanthuyne, in turn, reveals the potential of the photo book. There seems to be a new trend, the author feels, because more and more photographers are experimenting with the photo book, both in terms of form and content, in order to stretch the themes and boundaries of the documentary genre. They purposely use narrative and visual strategies. After all, photo books, with their striking attention to design, image selection, and order, are the perfect medium for telling complex and layered visual stories. Vanthuyne demonstrates this in interviews with photographers Laia Abril (Spain), Max Pinckers (Belgium) and Alejandro Cartagena (Mexico). On a level beyond the story, their photobooks are also a means to reflect on the current state of the media, visual culture as well as politics.

The relationship between staging and reality also runs like a thread through the work of Belgian art photographer Charlotte Lybeer, whose early focus was on the staged and controlled environments of gated communities and theme parks. She portrays people who define their identity through codes and masquerades, embracing a certain in-group membership while distancing themselves from mainstream society. She invited people in front of her camera who live their own fiction by transforming themselves into fantasy creatures. This time, Lybeer trains her lens on the influence of the culture of fear on the entertainment world. She offers insights into so-called preventive measures and simulations in order to eliminate potential dangers and to learn to protect herself against known and unknown threats.

Self-staging and the tension between parallel worlds also mark the conversation between artist Andrea Gorki and curator Ludovik Vermeersch. In 2015, the latter published *Personally, I'm Most Interested in the Shapes and Colours*. The book was accompanied by a ninety-minute lecture performance by Vermeersch himself, interweaving a theoretical reflection on the concept of 'transfigurative recontextualization' with a personal account of his manipulative collaboration with six young, Berlin-based artists. Gorki took this lecture performance as the starting point for a conversation with Vermeersch on the issues at stake in his work, notably the importance of authenticity for the attribution of agency to works of art, the dynamic between the self and the artist persona in both the appropriation of authorship and the assertion of authority, and the destabilizing effects on all of the above when deception is employed as an artistic strategy. The dialogue focused in particular on the use of alter egos, a recurring topic in Vermeersch's work.

In part three, *Imagining the Future*, the artists focus on what lies ahead of them. In particular, they investigate how fiction can be a useful instrument for imagining other, possible, future worlds and, hence, how it can affect the world today. This means entering the realm of speculative fiction, often regarded as a synonym for, or a subgenre of science fiction.[19] These artists are not looking for the actual or the factual, but for the possible, for what is thinkable or imaginable. After all, artists are in a privileged position to explore uncharted territories. Fiction and the imagination allow them to develop and try out new possibilities; not only conceptually–they draw up imaginary maps, make fictional sketches, develop alternative theories–but also in the form of imaginary perspectives that materialize into prototypes.

In a way, these projects are part of the 'commoning' movement, a new, practice-based ideology that is growing in the margins of society and the arts. The 'commons' is based on sharing, or on shared (intellectual) ownership and new social cooperatives, as is explained in the introduction to *Commonism*, a book with the telling subtitle *A New Aesthetics of the Real*, edited by Pascal Gielen and Nico Dockx. Their book aims to map this new 'self-conscious' ideology as well as the aesthetics that accompany it. Because, just like with other ideologies, it's about faith, according to the authors: 'a make-belief that claims reality' with an eye to imagining a better (utopian) future.[20] In *Commonism*, 'aesthetics of the real' is interpreted as 'a way of giving form to society and our contemporary human condition'.[21] Fiction and the imagination play a key role in this movement, which uses facts such as statistical knowledge about inequality as the starting point for solutions and scenarios for the future.

This cooperative spirit also underlies Platform Scenography, a Dutch network of scenographers and dramaturges. In her contribution, Sigrid Merx reports on their live research event in Athens, a city portrayed by the western media as the epicentre of a terrible economic crisis since 2010. For four days, a group of students, designers, and architects was sent off to explore specific spots in the city, looking for different realities and the relationships between them. The observations, ideas, and thoughts arising from these excursions were published live at the museum. The aim was to investigate whether it would be possible to charge the city with new meanings and to turn the setting of the economic crisis into a platform for renewal.

The relationship between the present, the past, and an imagined future also typifies the work of artist Elly Van Eeghem. Since 2012, she has been showing us urban development and the way cities change over time through her eyes and her lens. She operated from city districts in Paris, Berlin, Montreal, and Ghent, where she used photographs and videos, actions in public spaces as well as archival footage to engage in collective interventions with the local inhabitants. Via a multitude of sources she tries to offer a rich and varied look on what urbanization is and does. What does 'public' mean? Which parts of the city are public? Who is the public? How do you create a public? For this volume, Van Eeghem selected a series of archive images that encourage reflection on the city and the public space of today, with an eye to transitioning towards tomorrow.

Finally, Jonas Rutgeerts and Nienke Scholts' text focuses on our ability to imagine a different future and to actively regard that future as a plethora of possibilities. Even the prototype of a mobile robot that will patrol the European borders in the future affects our reality today. At least, that was the starting point for a two-year artistic research project initiated by Israeli choreographer Arkadi Zaides and his team. This research serves as the basis for Rutgeerts and Scholts' exploration of the possibilities that pre-enactment and speculation in dance and performance have to offer. If we want to steer clear of a future dictated by high-tech developers in Silicon Valley—a consumable futurism à la Elon Musk, that is—the authors argue that the question becomes: which future do we want to see 'performed'?

In an afterword to this book, Pascal Gielen reminds us that fiction, imagination and creativity are not only qualities of an artist. Even solid scientists must have a visionary spirit and be able to 'think the impossible' in order to be able to push the limits of our knowledge of reality. No hypothesis without imagination, no laboratory experiments without fictitious assumptions about reality. In short, fiction precedes facts. Art and science, but also fact and fiction are therefore not opposites. They are—also in the scientific realm—closely related.

The artists and authors in this book all ask questions about the shapes reality, the present, the past, and the future may take. Just like the editor, they do not adhere to a relative (postmodern) notion of truth, yet they do share a conviction that stories can represent worlds that we don't know yet.

Notes

1 Terry Eagleton, *The Event of Literature* (New Haven, CN: Yale University Press 2012), p. 106.
2 Bennison Gray, *The Phenomenon of Literature* (The Hague: Mouton, 1975), p. 117.
3 Eagleton, *The Event of Literature*, p. 112.
4 Ibid., p. 109.
5 Ibid., p. 112.
6 For more information on the double consciousness of the viewer and the aesthetic experience, see: Nele Wynants, *De binnenkant van het beeld: Immersie en theatraliteit in de kunsten* (Ghent: Mer Paper Kunsthalle, 2017).
7 Samuel T. Coleridge and William Wordsworth, *Lyrical Ballads: 1798 and 1800.* 1817, eds. Dahlia Porter and Michael Gamer (Ontario: Broadview Press, 2008), p. 470.
8 Kendall Walton, *Mimesis as Make-Believe: On the Foundations of the Representational Arts* (Cambridge, MA: Harvard University Press, 1990), p. 73.
9 Ibid., p. 34.
10 The same goes for documentary film and television. Back in the 1930s, John Grierson, pioneer of documentary cinema, already posited that a documentary is always a 'creative treatment of actuality'. For more on the evolution of the documentary genre, see: John Corner, *The Art of Record: A Critical Introduction to Documentary* (Manchester: Manchester University Press, 1996); and John Corner, 'Documentary Studies: Dimensions of Transition and Continuity', in *Rethinking Documentary: New Perspectives, New Practices*, eds. Wilma de Jong and Thomas Austin (Maidenhead: Open University Press, 2008), pp. 13–28.
11 Carol Martin, *Theatre of the Real* (Basingstoke: Palgrave Macmillan, 2013). For more information on contemporary documentary theatre, see: Alison Forsyth and Chris Megson, eds., *Get Real: Documentary Theatre Past and Present* (Basingstoke and New York: Palgrave Macmillan, 2009) and Thomas Irmer, 'A Search for New Realities: Documentary Theatre in Germany', *TDR* 50, no. 3 (2006), pp. 16–28.
12 Erika Fischer-Lichte, *The Transformative Power of Performance: A New Aesthetics* (London: Routledge 2008).
13 Hal Foster, 'An Archival Impulse', *October* 110 (Fall 2004), pp. 3–22, here p. 4.
14 Ibid., p. 3.
15 Sophie Berrebi, *The Shape of Evidence: Contemporary Art and the Document* (Amsterdam: Valiz, 2014).
16 Charlotte Aull Davies, *Reflexive Ethnography: A Guide to Researching Selves and Others* (New York: Routledge, 1999); Donna Haraway, 'Situated Knowledges: The Science Question in Feminism and the Privilege of Partial Perspective', *Feminist Studies* 14 (1988), pp. 575–599; Kurt Lewin, *Resolving Social Conflicts* (New York: Harper & Row, 1945).
17 Alun Munslow, *Narrative and History* (Houndsmills: Palgrave Macmillan, 2007).
18 For more on the artist's subjective perception and the performative abilities of the arts, see: Pascal Gielen and Nele Wynants, 'De queeste van de menswetenschappen: Lessen uit het onderzoek in de kunsten', *FORUM+* 25, no. 1 (30 March 2018), pp. 4–16, here p. 13. DOI: https://doi.org/10.5117/FORUM2018.1.GIEL. The English version of this article 'In Quest of the Humanities (Again): What we can learn from research in the arts' has been published in *Documenta tijdschrift voor theater* 35, no. 1 (2019), pp. 159–186.
19 Robert A. Heinlein (1949) is credited with coining the term, which twenty-first-century authors mainly use to distinguish themselves from mainstream science fiction and fantasy genres, and to break the conventions of these genres.
20 Pascal Gielen and Nico Dockx. *Commonism: A New Aesthetics of the Real* (Amsterdam: Valiz, 2018), p. 58.
21 Ibid.

Part 1

Reinventions of the Archive

Imaginations of Reality

Past, Present, and Future in a Fictional Framework

Nele Wynants

Fictional Museum

'Today I visited the fantastic exhibition by Thomas Bellinck–I highly recommend it!' Guy Verhofstadt tweeted on May 29, 2013. The leader of the ALDE group in the European Parliament's praise ensured the young artist plenty of media attention. In Bellinck's exhibition 'Domo de Eŭropa Historio en Ekzilo' visitors are taken over half a century into the future. There, from the perspective of the year 2063, they look back at the beginning of the twenty-first century. By depicting the rise, climax, and fall of the European Union the exhibition offers a disturbing retrospective on today's Europe. The exhibition was first set up in an empty building in Brussels' European Quarter, at a stone's throw from where the 'real' House of European History–a large museum of the history of the European Union–has meanwhile, in 2017, opened its doors. Bellinck made his own sassy interpretation of this theoretical exercise.

'Domo de Eŭropa Historio en Ekzilo' (House of European History in Exile) is a bureaucratic maze. Its form is reminiscent of an old-fashioned memorial museum. Visitors wander along dated display cases with dusty dolls, old maps, scale models and gadgets, such as a yellowed charter of the Nobel Peace Prize and framed guidelines on the minimum length of bananas, tomatoes, and leeks. In Esperanto, English, French, and Dutch, visitors can read how the EU period of 'Long Peace' was dominated by corruption, commercial lobbying, and self-interest. In spite of considerable efforts by European politicians to keep the Union together through trade agreements, legislation, and guidelines–which had to be translated into thirty different languages–it started to show cracks, and in Bellinck's 'museum of the future' the union eventually explodes somewhere in the 2060s. The museum is founded by the 'Friends of a Re-united Europe' as a memorial to this utopian European project.

The 'international exhibition about life in the former European Union' has since travelled to Rotterdam, Vienna, Athens, and Wiesbaden. Bellinck's museum was much acclaimed by the international press. 'An intelligent plea against rising nationalism and Euroscepticism without lapsing into Europropaganda', Dutch newspaper *de Volkskrant* wrote.[1] '[A] clever attempt to document the EU's current woes by constructing a fake museum of the future to examine what went wrong', said *The Guardian*.[2] In his exhibition Bellinck shows Europe's current transition by tracing the history of its origins. He starts in the past, travels to the present, and ends with a scenario for the future that might not be that far removed from the truth. He reminds us of old ideals, but also shows how these ideals have grown into grotesque realities with sometimes devastating effects, such as our European consumer behaviour. He also offers a critical take on the inhumanity of the current European migration policy. The exhibition is therefore not pure propaganda. Bellinck most cleverly shows how Europe finds itself at a turning point at the moment. Visitors are to draw a number of conclusions for themselves. In spite of the outright criticism on current European policy the exhibition also shows a strong urge to defend it. Are we willing to fight for a united Europe or will we let it disintegrate?

This is not Bellinck's first project in which he questions our current political situation. A recurring practice in this young body of work is the use of historical sources. These sources are placed in a fictional framework and reinterpreted. The performance *Lethal Inc.* (2011), for example, focused on the history of methods of execution, whereas his *Memento Park* (2015) examined the First World War commemoration industry. In all his projects Bellinck exposes how the past is connected to the future. Content determines form here: theatre, film, or exhibition. For 'Domo de Eŭropa Historio en Ekzilo' he chose a fictional museum, which offers visitors a futuristic perspective on a current reality.

Bellinck's work can be regarded as part of a wider trend among young Belgian artists who explicitly engage in a dialogue between reality and fiction, between past, present, and future. Elly van Eeghem and the brothers Chokri and Zouzou Ben Chikha in their projects also engage in an explicit relationship with historical, social, and political realities. However, we could also add artists such as Benjamin Verdonck, Jozef Wouters, and Simon Allemeersch to that list, to name but a few. They often leave the confines of existing art institutes to set up shop in public spaces or other social contexts. Elly van Eeghem, for example, is fascinated by urban development. She draws parallels between quarters in Paris, Berlin, and Montreal and those in her own hometown Ghent. Together with local residents and architects she examines existing urban plans and designs, and she works on alternative forms of urban living for the future. Chokri and Zouzou Ben Chikha (Action Zoo Humain) took the Ghent World Fair of 1913 as their starting point. More than 150 Senegalese and Filipinos were exhibited for six months in reconstructed African villages where they had to re-enact authentic scenes for an amused white audience. Precisely one hundred years later, Action Zoo Humain established a Truth Commission to indict the impact of our colonial past on the present. The experiment was repeated in Kaapstad (2014), Antwerp (2016), Mechelen (2017), and Brussels (2018) where the Truth Commission convened in the old Antwerp Palace of Justice, the Mechelse city hall Council room, and the Belgian Senate, respectively.[3]

In spite of the diversity of projects these artists share some common ground. They all create a tension between fiction and reality in their work and dissociate themselves from standard art formats: it's not theatre, an installation, or an exhibition in the strictest sense of those words. Instead, Bellinck, Van Eeghem, and Action Zoo Humain develop artistic forms they derive from the social context in which they take up residence: the model of the museum, the model of the urban development project, the model of the courthouse. Since this historical, social and political reality as original source material lies at the foundation of these projects, they have decidedly documentary characteristics. And yet this is not documentary art. These artists translate the archival sources, oral testimonies, or historical plans they use into an artistic context. They place their historical sources in a fictional framework and thereby intentionally obscure the demarcation lines between fiction and reality. This translation has a distinctly critical potential, but doesn't aim at an objective truth, nor a historically correct representation of the past. What these artists do, is inspire different depictions of the reality in which they take up residence.

City of the Future

It's significant that this group of young artists choose the city—and by extension the public space—as their workplace. They try to find a place where they, while interacting with their surroundings, can question and put into practice such concepts as urbanity, public spaces, and activism. The focal point in their work is the question of how they can think about the world they want to live in. With their artistic practice they try to anchor themselves explicitly in society. In that sense working in public spaces makes perfect sense. Not because they want to escape from the institutional borders of the established institutes, like the avant-garde artists in the 1920s and 1960s. The current generation of artists cleverly use the institutional frameworks they are offered. Often social criticism frameworks are in part co-developed by the big subsidized cultural institutions.

Elly van Eeghem, for example, is one of five so-called City Residents who have been supported by arts centre Vooruit in Ghent since August 2012. By engaging a group of young artists with different artistic backgrounds in a dialogue in public spaces, Vooruit stimulates the City Residents to develop a joint discourse around art and society. In that context Van Eeghem explores depictions of urban planning in her long running project *(Dis)Placed Interventions*. She focuses on places in Belgium as well as abroad that are going through a radical physical or social change and translates her insights into new urban and social models. She studies their history and talks to the local residents. Using these different sources, the young artist makes a performance, film, installation, or exhibition in which she always makes a connection to the present.

In 2015 Van Eeghem worked in the Ghent district of Malem. Together with a group of residents she developed alternative forms of housing for this quarter, which is under threat because of rising water levels. Van Eeghem combines a very real threat to the island (humidity of the housing blocks) with a fictional worst-case scenario (the island will be flooded soon). They joined forces with a team of architects in a Laboratorium voor de Ontwikkeling van het Nieuwe Wonen (Laboratory for the Development of New Urban Living), LOW for short, a think tank that devises innovative residential models tailored to the Malem district and the future city. Here the residents designed innovative forms of housing for the city of tomorrow. The residents acted as contractor and searched for potential investors in the development and execution of a first prototype. During *Plan Malem (Topography of the Island State)* interested parties were given a tour and were afterwards invited to support the project financially and thus be a shareholder in securing their own future. What started as a utopian laboratory for new forms of housing evolved into a very real investigation into current themes such as privatization, urban development, and the future of council housing.

These engaged projects can of course be situated in a long tradition of artistic movements that explore the boundaries between play and reality by intervening in public spaces artistically and thus explicitly strengthening the connection between art and life. The street has always been a popular field of action and subject for artists. In the 1960s, Guy Debord and his Situationist

International already wanted to critically question existing social conditions. Debord's agenda was explicitly political. The same goes for Brazilian theatre practitioner Augusto Boal's Invisible Theatre in the 1970s. Through 'invisible' actions in public spaces Boal wanted to emancipate his oblivious audience. Unlike their radical predecessors, Elly van Eeghem and Thomas Bellinck's motivations are less didactical. They do not aim for a social revolution or the emancipation of the working classes, but rather want to find forms of expression that question the current system by highlighting alternative depictions. They place a social reality in a theatrical framework. At the same time, they take the liberty to fictionalize this social, historical and political reality (in this case the museum, the urban development project, the courthouse). In this way the artists mock social frameworks and play games with the expectations of the spectator.

Dramaturg Sébastien Hendrickx called this the 'pretend strategy'. In his text 'Kunst die zich voordoet alsof ze iets anders is dan kunst' (Art that pretends to be something other than art), the author discusses several projects in which he himself was involved as a dramaturge. He situates these projects in what he calls a 'social avant-garde', a broad social movement that criticizes the status quo and experiments with alternative future imaginations.[4] Therefore, the artists he discusses use the 'pretend strategy'. According to Hendrickx, this artistic strategy follows a double logic. On the one hand an artist takes place in a specific social environment (the museum, the urban development project, the court) and imitates the conventions, the roles, and the discourse specific to that environment. On the other hand, this practice is introduced into the domain of art, where–free of its own conventions–it can be manipulated and questioned. This strategy allows artists an enormous formal freedom. They can embrace the heteronomy, and freely make use of the roles, activities, procedures, discourses, attributes, and spaces that characterize other social practices.

Courthouse of the Past

With a third example I would like to show that these artists' practices can have a direct impact on reality and the history they relate to. On April 10, 2013, in a striking video message, the mayor of Ghent Daniël Termont offered his apologies for humiliating the people of Senegal and the Philippines at the 1913 World Fair. No less than 128 Senegalese and 60 Filipinos were exhibited as an exotic curiosum in recreated African villages in Ghent. The Senegalese and Filipinos were part of a travelling circus for the entertainment of the white Westerner. After the fair closed, these people wandered around the streets of Ghent for a month. They received 10 Belgian francs for their services, about a third of a working monthly wage back then. The illustrious Belgian writer Cyriel Buysse described them at the time as 'the result of cross-breeding monkeys with Mongols'.[5]

The cause of the mayor's apology to the descendants of the victims was the Truth Commission. This Commission was founded exactly hundred years after the fact by Action Zoo Humain, the theatre company led by Chokri and Zouzou Ben Chikha. The commission explored the effect of this colonial past on the present. In cooperation with the descendants of Madi Diali, a Senegalese who didn't survive the 'human zoo', the company examined what had happened exactly by recreating the facts in court in the presence of a commission of experts. The commission's activities could be followed in the old palace of justice in Ghent. In this way the project took the shape of a legal session chaired by former Province Governor Herman Balthazar.

The complicated relationship between reality and the staging of the project was very clearly analyzed by dramaturg Ivo Kuyl.[6] He emphasized the 'realistic effect' of the setting (the courthouse) and the fact that 'real politicians', 'real Senegalese people' and 'real academic experts' took part.[7] Great pains were taken to make the spectator forget this was fiction, says Kuyl. At the same time the spectator is constantly reminded everything is staged. First by the Ben Chikha brothers, who act as court security officers. Next by actor Mourade Zeguendi, who protests indignantly from the audience about the fact that the audience is entertained during the intermission by a spectacular dance group of Senegalese dancers. Actress Marijke Pinoy in turn criticizes the choice to have African dancer Chantal Loial dance behind a glass wall; once more she is exhibited in a colonial perspective.

Multiple Perspectives

With these artistic interventions Action Zoo Humain cleverly encourages reflection on how reality shows itself to us in and by its staging. The spectator is constantly confronted with different perspectives on the situation and is actively challenged during that game. Just as in Elly van Eeghem and Thomas Bellinck's projects, the line between reality and fiction, between reality and staging, is very thin. Action Zoo Humain even deliberately tries to blur this line and make the resulting confusion the subject of the project. The playing with stereotypes and constant undermining of the spectator's expectations provide a multiple perspective on the colonial past and its effect on the present.

This complexity is perhaps most visible in the dancing body of Chantal Loial. On the one hand, this dancer represents the stereotype black dancing body as a spectacle. At the same time, Loial is very conscious of her role and plays an ambiguous game with the process of stereotyping. Her dancing body intertwines the past, the present, and the future. After her ambiguous dance she also takes place in the audience to follow the further course of the process. In this way she turns the game of looking and being looked at around and undermines the binary oppositions that are inherent to postcolonial thinking (we-she, perpetrator-victim, past-present). The result is not so much a moralizing political condemnation but rather exposes the complexity of the postcolonial debate. Through the format of a Truth Commission, placed in a theatrical framework, the makers question the obvious truth regimes, the truth commission as legal apparatus, and the status of the witness or the historical source in their historical contexts.

In this sense, this project, just as much as the work of Elly Van Eeghem and Thomas Bellinck, can be considered as a form of what Carol Martin calls 'theatre of the real'.[8] This is not documentary theatre in the strict sense of the word. Martin's term refers to theatre models that relate to reality in very different ways. The author discusses a wide range of examples with the most important common objective 'to intend for spectators to reconsider the world around them on the basis of the theatrical experiences these works offer'.[9] The 'theatre of the real' approaches reality through a self-conscious interweaving of fiction and non-fiction. Thus, according to Martin, that theatre becomes a relevant source of information that can contribute in a meaningful way to how we frame, view, and review reality through 'acts of imagination'.[10]

Elly van Eeghem, Thomas Bellinck and Action Zoo Humain indeed focus explicitly on the impact of the past on the social and political truths of today. They are not striving for an objective reality; rather, they want to expose a forgotten history, a place or a community. They don't claim any truth, probability, or answer, but depict reality in different possible ways. These artists translate snippets of memories, moments of the collective past, but also new possibilities for the future to an artistic universe. In this way they offer different, multiple perspectives on reality. Mixed with depictions of reality they feed a multi-facetted reflection on the past. At the same time their interventions stimulate a critical relation to the present and open up alternative possibilities for the future.

With this text Nele Wynants received the second prize for young dutch art criticism 2016, category essay. It's an abridged version of an article published in dutch in march 2016 in *FORUM⁺ voor onderzoek en kunsten - for research and art.* A copy of the article is on the website of the international association of art critics (http://aicainternational.Org).

Notes

1 Leen Vervaeke, 'Terugblik uit 2063: Hoe EU kapotging', *de Volkskrant*, 4 June 2013, p. 15.
2 Ian Traynor, 'EU will collapse in 2018, according to "museum of the future" art project', *The Guardian*, 9 May 2013. All reviews of this project can be found on the website of the Brussels City Theatre KVS: www.kvs.be/nl/producties/domo-de-europa-historio-en-ekzilo (accessed 20 December 2018).
3 For more information on this project, see www.actionzoohumain.be.
4 Sébastien Hendrickx, 'Kunst die zich voordoet alsof ze iets anders is dan kunst', *Rekto:verso* no. 58, 2013, n.p., www.rektoverso.be.
5 Cited on the website of Action Zoo Humain: www.actionzoohumain.be.
6 Ivo Kuyl, 'De Waarheidscommissie: Expo Zoo Humaine van Chokri en Zouzou Ben Chikha', *Etcetera* 31, no. 133 (2013), pp. 55–57.
7 Ibid., p. 56.
8 Carol Martin, *Theatre of the Real* (Basingstoke: Palgrave Macmillan, 2013).
9 Ibid., p. 175.
10 Ibid., p. 74.

Screening the City
The Role of the Brussels Archive in the Found-Footage Film Night Has Come

Peter Van Goethem

Brussels Captured on Film

To celebrate the 25th anniversary of the Brussels capital region, the Royal Belgian Film Archive Cinematek released the DVD *Brussel gefilmde stad* (Brussels captured on film) in 2014. The large selection of archival footage on this DVD includes the earliest images of the city shot by cameraman Alexandre Promio in 1897 (images commissioned by Lumière) and spans almost the entire twentieth century. With this careful selection, the editors aimed at a representative image of the history of Brussels throughout the past century. As a member of the editorial team, and in preparation for this DVD, I frequently visited the Cinematek's movie depot in Elsene. For two years I immersed myself in Brussels' film archive. Not all of the archival footage has been restored or is available for viewing, but the Brussels cinematic memory that is accessible and has been documented contains no less than 1268 films (mainly non-fictional) that deal directly or indirectly with the city. In addition to avantgarde experiments (8 films), recordings of events (8 films), promotional films (11 films), and amateur recordings (20 films), the lion's share consists of reports (135 films) and journalistic productions (531 films), educational (65 films), propaganda (86 films) or documentary films (288 films), and films commissioned by the government and by companies wanting to provide information on their products or services (116 films). The vast majority of these audio-visual products was created at the height of modernity in Brussels, from the 1920s till the 1970s.

In the next phase, assuming the role of researcher/film director, I took on the challenge of selecting and reusing the archival material from that very same audio-visual database to artistically reinterpret the history of Brussels, namely in a found footage film entitled *Night Has Come* (2018).

As an editor/archivist working on the DVD *Brussel gefilmde stad*, I made a selection that portrays the history of Brussels both historically and aesthetically. In the context of the film *Night Has Come*, as a researcher and a filmmaker, I had recourse to found footage image technologies such as repetition, flashback, voiceover and sampling, in order to move away from the original meaning and create new meanings based on a self-written script. When selecting films for the DVD, I maintained a cautious approach, putting the historical material first and presenting it in terms of its historical and informative value. When making the film, by contrast, I shone an investigative light on the source material by dusting off the footage, slowly excavating it (like an archaeologist would), trimming off excess material and trying–probing and searching–to find the possible and hidden meanings the images might still carry or evoke outside their historical context.

The idea of reusing existing audio-visual material and setting it in a new context is the common denominator of all found footage films.[1] It's what sets them apart from other audio-visual genres such as documentaries and journalism, which use existing images as proof or illustration. In the latter case, the objectivity and truthfulness of the story of the initial context often depends on the footage.

The movie *Night Has Come* alternates between Belgian amateur filmmaker Raymond Devaux' footage and that of historical events that took place in Brussels. Using the city's imagined historical reality, the movie weaves the selected archival footage into a new, fictional story based on a self-written filmscript. To begin with, the fragments about Brussels were decontextualized: they are disengaged from their original source, but also disengaged from their time and their particular historical aesthetics. Yet, at the same time, the memory of the source material lingers on in the images. The viewer shifts between an awareness of the source and the new usage, the new story.

Consisting of a selection of film fragments, the movie feels like a patchwork of the protagonist's memories and makes the mounting tension between the government and its citizens tangible. Urban images of Brussels depict the real memories as well as the dystopian present in the movie, while Devaux' film recordings portray the memories that have been manipulated by the government. Devaux' amateur movies do not feature significant sites or famous people, but mainly portray happy and personal events–which the movie interprets as the protagonist's artificial childhood memories. Focusing as they do on the incidental, the everyday, and the ahistorical, these film fragments belong squarely in Paula Amad's counter-archive.

To form a picture of the development of the Brussels cityscape, I eventually selected 21 archive films with the help of the rest of the editorial team. Our selection included films by famous Belgian professional and amateur documentary makers such as Jean Harlez (1924) and Charles Dekeukeleire (1905–1971). Various cinematographers have devoted themselves to depicting the Brussels cityscape, and their movies offer a glimpse into a period of massive change, from the emergence of Brussels as a major city at the end of the nineteenth century until its appearance on the international scene as a full-blown metropolis. We selected and categorized the archival material according to three socio-political tendencies that adequately sum up the transition and transformation of Brussels throughout the fast-paced twentieth century: modernization, internationalization, and Europeanization. Each of these phases has been crucial in shaping the city's urban, political, and social tissue, making Brussels the metropolis we know today. The DVD connects these phases with the help of films depicting historical facts and social phenomena such as the fragmentation of the city, the sense of alienation among its residents and visitors alike, and the rise and fall of the optimism of progress.[2]

In this article I will discuss these two roles as two seemingly contrasting but closely connected ways of dealing with historical films as sources. At the same time, this will allow me to reflect on the function of the archive and the (cultural) memory.

Found Footage

Found footage film as a genre touches the essence of a much wider–and at first glance unrelated–practice of film archiving,[3] which is synonymous with collecting, preserving, and presenting our cinematic heritage, often with the purpose of restoring the films in question and transferring them onto new media and digital formats, hence making them available for screening again. In addition, film archiving is about showing films in a new context. Archival footage makes its way to the big screen in museums, movie theatres, and other public spaces. Television broadcasts, DVDs, online platforms, and mobile devices also help to keep the cinematic heritage alive, bring it to the wider world and activate it. Regardless of how a movie archive breathes new life into its collection or presents it with a contemporary twist, it remains loyal to the original, both from a historical and an aesthetic point of view. Yet no matter how faithfully film archivists go about their job, restoring and digitally presenting cinematic heritage inevitably entails a decontextualization. Whenever a copy of an archive film is projected via another technological device than the one that was originally used, and in another time, the film ceases to function as a primary source. Moreover, according to Marie-Anne Chabin, archives cannot but paint a distorted picture of reality, given the materiality of the filmic documents and the fact that it matters how things are captured or represented.[4] When selecting and (re)-presenting audio-visual archival items, the practice of the movie director becomes entangled with that of the film archivist, because, in a way, they both decontextualize the material they work with.

Raymond Devaux' Home Movies

While browsing the Cinematek's archive, the home movies by amateur director Raymond Devaux immediately captured my attention. Belonging to the Brussels movie canon, Devaux' home movies nevertheless failed to make it into the core collection and the eventual DVD selection for *Brussel gefilmde stad* because their audio-visual mark is but a footnote in the history of Brussels. Devaux' films peek inside the private life of the average middle-class household, which is dotted with family outings, family parties, first and solemn communions, and weddings. The camera captured these ordinary events as personal memories, presenting a private history rather than contributing to the construction of the public history of Brussels. Because they are so recognizable, Devaux' films manage to pull the past on top of the present. They are timeless and universal. Almost all of us can relate to them and identify with the main characters. It is as if the images are representations of a kind of life that belongs to all of us.[5] This effect is heightened by the illusion of truth that the films sustain, by our willingness as viewers to believe in this footage and to accept its authenticity.

As a researcher/archivist, I ran into the limits of the DVD-project, which were determined by its particular set-up. After all, the initial goal of depicting the development of the Brussels cityscape throughout the twentieth century in order to expand and deepen the viewer's knowledge and understanding of the past, failed to take into account the personal characteristics and visions of individuals films such as Devaux' home movies. Given that the latter did not end up in the DVD's core collection and that the historical material selected for the DVD is but a snapshot of a particular moment in time that, more than anything else, reflects the archive-selector's choices, the home movies presented a challenge to the practices of the film archive and the way it deals with its collection on Brussels. A key question for the film archive concerns its relation to memory. If archives are the memory of a society, then whose memory are they, in fact?[6] The archive can keep the audio-visual memory of Brussels alive or activate it. Yet it can also contribute to memory loss by sealing off its contents, preventing footage from being remembered. This begs the question: is something archived because of its historical value, or does an archive item derive its value from the fact that is it archived? This would mean that the power of the memories of a city such as Brussels lie in the film archive itself, and that the latter plays a crucial role in facilitating the process of remembrance.

As a filmmaker, I could explore the boundaries of Brussels' cinematographic past in my artistic investigation, and try to find another way to open up the city's archival material to the public. I started from the idea that the filmic past is always a past in which personal and historical time converge and where 'personal, social and political contexts intersect and determine the meaning of the past'.[7] The practices of the film archivist challenged me in my role as a filmmaker looking for archive films that tend to lay bare the limits of traditional archival practices, but the reverse was also true: the filmmaker in me challenged the film archivist by questioning the institutional role of archives in storing, unlocking, and describing movie history.

The archive films about Brussels at Cinematek are a source of knowledge about the past. The added value of Devaux' movies as historical sources in my film does not lie in their evidential value regarding historical events, but in their memory value. By cataloguing everyday life, Devaux' films record the memory of daily life and transform memories into personal facts. The home movies thus call into question what Paula Amad has labelled the 'positivist archival impulse'. In her book *Counter-Archive: Film, the Everyday, and Albert Kahn's Archives de la Planète* (2010), she interprets the emergence of cinematography as a challenge to the text-based archive in its desire for order, coherence, and objectivity. Movies could store the present for future reference, in science or education: 'Like the French banker Albert Kahn who ordered recordings to be made all over the world for his "archive of the planet", and like fathers who used a camera to capture their family's stories.'[8]

Amad testifies to the (im)possibility of creating order in this vast amount of image data. Fragmentation, unpredictability, and a lack of clarity are all necessarily accepted as characteristics of the archive. In the act of archiving, these counter-archivist characteristics 'have no utilitarian or evidentiary purpose, but merely exist to be forgotten, due to their focus on the incidental, the everyday, the non-essential information'.[9] For Amad, the counter-archive—

to which Devaux' home movies also belong–does not stand outside the inventory, but offers an alternative way to open up the archive. Showing that an historical event can be seen from different angles, they provide another perspective on the phenomenon of memory and the construction of history.

Night Has Come

Night Has Come starts from a fictional main character's personal quest for himself and his past. This protagonist is an anonymous old man who is a patient in a sanatorium at an unspecified location. He suffers from a kind of amnesia induced by a virus. The infection spreads and the *Night* is near: a dystopian period for humankind in which collective amnesia rules supreme and the past crumbles due to people's inability to produce any memories.

The government steps in and scientists are ordered to find a cure for the virus. At first, a vaccination programme is successfully set up; it seems the perfect antidote. Yet slowly but surely, people begin to revolt against the treatment and the vaccinations. They start questioning the authenticity of their own memories, while growing increasingly conscious of another truth–namely, that *Night* is a fictional construct meant to spread fear and panic in the face of a potential danger. The other truth is that the presence of the virus is tolerated by a government that is not immediately visible nor recognizable, but uses the treatment to manipulate its citizens: their memories are artificially implanted to create the reality that the government wants them to remember. These artificial memories are meant to suppress authentic memories and, eventually, gain control over humankind and crush all resistance.

By spreading the virus, the government uses fear as a political tool. By demanding that the memories of its citizens are stored and made available for government scrutiny, the authorities appropriate the memories of the people. Whoever refuses the treatment or raises objections, is persecuted. Control and militarization, creating order to maintain or restore safety: a society in a high state of readiness and exceptionalism is a recurring motif in history.

To illustrate the main character's authentic (as opposed to implanted) memories, the film reorganizes the cinematographic past of Brussels and strips the selected archival footage of its original historical context as well as of its makers' intentions. The past that gets represented–the historical events, locations and buildings–becomes a part of the memory patchwork created by the film. The way in which this patchwork of the protagonist's memories is visually edited in the film not only serves the narrative, but also functions as a metaphor for the way human memory itself works. The protagonist's memory is not unambiguous in the movie. His memories take root in selection, distortion, fragmentation, repetition, and blurring–processes that are mirrored in the editing, which is done associatively rather than chronologically (see also note 1).

In addition, the memory patchwork points to a connection between the uncertain status of a memory and that of archival footage. The degree of realism ascribed to all archival footage assumes the status of a memory. This is not an historically factual memory, but one that belongs to a failing brain in which the past of Brussels serves an evocative function. By allowing openness and refusing to hermetically seal stories, by rearranging and juxtaposing various film fragments, the selected archival footage illustrates the idea that history does not unfold according to definite laws and chronologies, with an end goal in mind, but rather explores the boundaries of history as well, to paraphrase historian Robert A. Rosenstone.[10] The viewer loses historical awareness, and in case they recognize something, they only see a reflection of the original historical facts, so that they can gain a new or other perspective on the past.

The absence of a traditional linear narrative caused by a multitude of visions and dreams, the contradictions that arise from doubts about the status of memories (authentic or artificial), and the deliberate fragmentation of visual material: these characteristics do not undermine the movie or the history of the city of Brussels that it is devoted to. Rather, they have a well-defined function: to introduce the idea that, in addition to facts, fiction and memory can make substantial contributions to historical discussions. Thus, the movie recognizes that history is always partial, and that personal, social, and political contexts also determine the interpretation of the past.[11]

To Conclude

Personal and historical time, authentic and artificial memories come together in *Night Has Come*, yet their relationship in the movie is tense. Memory as a metaphor equals memory as conflict. By reorganizing and reinterpreting Brussels' cinematographic heritage, the movie aims to provide a contemporary comment on the movie archive itself. After all, the movie archive is an equally uncertain memory in which a microscopic virus–that of the decontextualization of its contents–generates new meanings that change over time. What seems to be a steady and factual collection is in fact intrinsically impure and uncertain, and just like our memory it depends on the stories that the images are woven into. By radicalizing this idea, the movie problematizes the status of the film archive. The found footage film *Night Has Come* therefore invites us to rethink the practice of archiving films, in particular the way an archive interacts with its contents and the past. It's an invitation to expand the role of the film archivist or film scientist, to go beyond dusting off the past and to creatively explore and question the borders of this past.

Notes

1 The reuse and adaptation of existing images and sounds has been artistically interpreted in many ways throughout the history of cinema: from surrealist and experimental short films such as *Rose Hobart* (Joseph Cornell, 1936) to movies like *Lyrisch nitraat* (Peter Delpeut, 1991) and *Decasia* (Bill Morrison, 2001), which pay tribute to the beauty of decaying archival material. On the other hand, with their movies based on media imagery, media makers such as Jayne Loader, Kevin and Pierce Rafferty (*Atomic Café*, 1982), Craig Baldwin (*Tribulation 99*, 1992) and Johan Grimonprez (*Dial H-I-S-T-O-R-Y*, 1997) put up critical resistance to the way images are used in mainstream media and communication. Yet another approach can be found in movies made from fragments of fictional films, like *Dead Men Don't Wear Plaid* (Carl Reiner, 1982). And, lastly, there are movies such as *Free Fall* (Péter Forgács, 1996), *The Maelstrom: A Family Chronicle* (Péter Forgács, 1997), *Capturing the Friedmans* (Andrew Jarecki, 2003) and *The Windmill Movie* (Alexander Olch, 2008), which use amateur films to recount life stories and make the past tangible.

2 For more information on the cinematic representation of Brussels throughout the twentieth century see: Peter Van Goethem, 'Screening the City: Reading Brussels' Urban Landscape Through Historic Non-Fiction Film Footage', in *Evaluating Art and Design Research: Reflections, Evaluation Practices and Research Presentations*, ed. Walter Ysebaert and Binke Van Kerckhoven (Brussels: VUB Press, 2018), as well as the DVD *Brussel gefilmde stad* (Cinematek Brussels 2018).

3 Giovanna Fossatti, 'Found Footage: Filmmaking, Film Archiving and New Participatory Platforms' in *Found Footage: Cinema Exposed*, eds. Marente Bloemheuvel, Giovanna Fossatti and Jaap Guldemond (Amsterdam: Amsterdam University Press, 2012), p. 178.

4 Quoted in: Annemieke de Jong, *Het boek van zand: Naar een ontologie van het digitale archief* (Hilversum: Nederlands Instituut voor Beeld en Geluid, 2006), p. 13.

5 Hungarian filmmaker Péter Forgács, who frequently used home movies, once confessed that after every project he ended up feeling as if the amateur movie-makers had shared their memories with him for a while: 'To my knowledge, these kinds of home movies are the best way to dive into the past', Forgács said, adding: 'Imagine there would be home movies from the seventeenth century!' (Henk van Gelder, 'Met familiefilmpjes teruggaan in de tijd', *NRC Handelsblad*, 3 May 1997).

6 De Jong, *Het boek van zand*, pp. 13-14.

7 Robert A. Rosenstone, *Visions of the Past: The Challenge of Film to Our Idea of History* (Cambridge, MA: Harvard University Press, 1995), p. 61.

8 Susan Aasman, *Ritueel van huiselijk geluk: Een cultuurhistorische verkenning van de familiefilm* (Amsterdam: Het Spinhuis, 2004), p. 49.

9 Jan-Christopher Horak, 'Counter-Archive: Film, the Everyday, and Albert Kahn's Archives de la Planète' (review), *Screening the Past* (screeningthepast.com), 2011.

10 Robert A. Rosenstone, 'The Future of the Past: Film and the Beginnings of Postmodern History', in *The Persistence of History: Cinema, Television and the Modern Event*, ed. Vivian Carol Sobchack (New York: Routledge, 1996), pp. 205-207.

11 Ibid., pp. 207-215.

The Private Collection of Acácio Nobre
Homo Universalis of the Portuguese Avant-garde

Patrícia Portela

The Private Collection of Acácio Nobre is the result of sixteen years of researching, collecting, following the clues, and imagining what my country would be like today if this outstanding unknown man would have realized some of his inventions, educational projects, and political ideas.

Based on Acácio Nobre's unfinished works and sketched ideas I have constructed several artistic projects, such as a sound installation at the National Museum of Contemporary Art in Lisbon (MNAC), a concert-performance for a typewriter and a keyboard that travelled around Europe, and a book in which part of his estate is described, presented, and reflected on.

Curiously enough, for almost two decades the question around this Portuguese personality is about the veracity of the documents and the plausibility of their existence. Well, how can one answer those questions about a man who did not seem to accomplish most of the projects he dreamt of during his time, although most of his ideas are today, in one way or another, part of our society and have been realized in our schools, gardens, philosophical schools?

Does he now exist because somehow, we managed to assemble his work? Does he now exist because his projects have been realized although not by him? Does he now exist because he has physically existed, although no one seemed to have noticed him at the time he was alive?

The Estate of Acácio Nobre

> 'An estate is worth nothing if we do not know who it belongs to, if we do not recognize its value. What we do not know, we do not have.'[1]

In 1999 I discovered, in my grandparents' cellar, a chest filled with texts and plans belonging to Acácio Nobre (1869–1968), a man of note in the nineteenth century for whom it was a burden to be alive for much of the twentieth century. A man who was silenced by a dictatorship and eliminated from (almost) all historical records. In the chest I found:

543 letters (some sent—copies on carbon paper—others not), loose notes, draft plans, 1 notebook without dates, 1 scrapbook with dates, 3 packets of Fentanyl, 1 compass, 12 prototypes of games for children and adults, 1 manifesto in code, 88 drafts of letters to ministers, secretaries of State and members of the Council of the Crown, 1 membership card for the FANC.

All of this aroused my curiosity about a period that has always fascinated me. Such an obscure author does not appear on Google.

Estate AN/1

My Grandmother's FANC membership card

FANC–Friends of Acácio Nobre Club, founded in 1952, its members being various illustrious and intellectual figures from different countries and periods.

Objectives:

a) The recognition and recovery of the Acácio Nobre Estate.
b) To make certain that his works remain scattered and likely to be lost so they can be found time and time again.

Estate AN/2

Internal Regulation of the FANC, document dated 1952.

c) No member of the FANC may have more than three objects belonging to Acácio Nobre in his possession at any one time. All objects that exceed the permitted number should be auctioned, donated, given, or recycled into new works by other authors.

In an initial phase I limited myself to following the clues left by each object and/or document found in the estate. This was how I found the Report N° 453/07 of the geometric operation of the PGICS–General Police for Information of a Secret Nature, later called PIDE, International Police of the Defence of the State, the dictatorship's main tool of repression. It was thanks to the efforts by a legal foundation of the FANC that the interest of PIDE in Acácio Nobre was rekindled. Today, the reports by PIDE are the only official records of Acácio Nobre's life beyond the above-mentioned estate. Those records were the first pieces of a puzzle, the beginning of Ariadne's thread.

Excerpt of Report 453/07 (PIDE)
(Torre do Tombo Archive, Lisbon)

António dos Santos, undercover officer n° 1324/007

'I infiltrated the FANC, as a member, at 8.34 p.m. on the 23rd of April 1953. In this club everyone introduces himself by his first name only (false, I suspect) and follows the same dress code: a white tie. It is a point of honour neither to be recognized nor photographed.'

Estate AN/0006

Facsimile and transcription of rough sketch of Acácio Nobre's letter to João Franco,2 Secretary of State and member of the Council of the Crown, Paris, 22nd of October 1890.

Esteemed Secretary of State and member of the Council of the Crown João Franco,

I hereby humbly present to you my plans for the implementation of an innovative method of educating the children and workers of Portugal. The Froebel Kindergarten Programme is based on the spontaneous instinct of the baby (and the human being in general) towards construction and creativity. Whereas, in the early part of this century, the child had to assume the behaviour of the adult, supported in figurative play and imitating society, playing at kitchens, or knights in shining armour, or soldiers, or kings, or doctors or mummies and daddies, the alternative games and the drawing methods of Froebel intend to promote the skill, the dexterity and consequently the self-confidence of the young, with the intention of preparing lucid and skilled citizens and thus contributing to a magnificent future working class. Allow me to be so bold as to believe that Portugal, a rural and traditionalist country, which has some difficulty in finding its way to modernity, may and indeed should participate in this process of[3]

Estate AN/3

Promotional Leaflet on glossy paper, for Richter & Co, 1900

Richter & Co were the representatives of Froebel's Kindergarten Gift Boxes for the whole of Europe and world leader in the sale of geometric puzzles. Acácio Nobre was their most active collaborator for more than fifteen years.

Estate AN/4–Tangram

Seven triangular pieces made of quartz sand, linseed and olive oil with which all of the shapes of Nature can be formed. This Chinese game, father of all puzzles, was brought to Europe in 1817 by Damázio Nobre, and to America by captain Von Gonidor of the same ship in which Nobre was sailing. The captain acquired a tangram made of carved ivory while the sailor and whale catcher purchased one with wooden pieces; the first one travelled to the Americas where it was given as a gift to an aristocratic American lady from Philadelphia, the latter arrived in the Azores and was given to his son, one day to be the father of Acácio Nobre. In 1818, the tangram was Richter & Co's greatest sales success.

Estate AN/5—Plan N° 44/08 Volleyscope
Volleyball game for two made from a military oscilloscope and two joysticks. Dated 1920.[4]

Estate AN/6
Ovoid Puzzle, wooden prototype, 1918
The first toy Acácio Nobre invented for Richter & Co: a deceptively simple masterpiece, which can be dismantled into more than a hundred pieces and which, in various combinations, can shape the forms of many different birds.

Estate AN/345
Rudolstadt, 27th of April 1891
Esteemed Secretary of State and Minister of Public Instruction and Fine Arts, João Franco,

I write to you of my plans to establish the Froebel Institute in our country. It is the growing desire of various pedagogues, throughout the whole of Europe, to offer the study of drawing to all and not only to artists and the wealthy aristocracy. In order for drawing to reach the hands of all of those who intend to occupy their time with the progress of society, new drawing conventions have been studied and tried out. It is indisputable that the simplification of the representation of Nature through Geometry has had an excellent effect on the development of the world's major powers. And why? Because a good worker is he who has good vision, and the principles of intuitive vision are: primarily the straight line and then the square. From the subdivision of a square, all shapes are possible. And the division of the square is the multiplication of the triangle. And the multiplication of the triangle is the secret of modernity in its new two-dimensional representation, the reinstitution of Plato's solids. When a man knows how to draw a cone, a cube and a sphere to perfection, he has command over the whole of the forms of Nature in all its complexity. It is no more than mastery of the Universe that we offer, with the teaching of drawing for all.[5]

Estate AN/0003
Things to do: rewrite promotional leaflet. Introduce puzzle 3 into machine 12. Write to Alva. Not forget visit Albert E. Letter to

Secretary of State, which may begin thus: In June 1729 Jonathan Swift wrote: 'When a true genius appears in the world, you may know him by this sign, that the clowns are all in confederacy against him.' But, believe you me, esteemed Secretary of State, clowns we are not, we both know that progress comes with the changing of conventions, that the worst threat of all is the freezing of ideas, paralysis before change is fatal. Froebelian schools exist since 1877 in Moscow, Kiev, Riga, St Petersburg, and even in Japan. Only a childhood educated along new and transgressive guidelines can produce a significant change in society in the coming centuries. I am aware that what I am asking you is radical, but accept my challenge, abandon all former concepts and embrace the unknown with all your strength. I trust that you know as well as I that revolution is the substitution of the elite. A monarchy is not destroyed by the dethroning of a king only. True revolution is that of mentalities.[6] What I am in fact asking you, esteemed Secretary of State, is that you maximize the exposure of the country to the effects of the *black swan* and to the transmission of anti-knowledge, thus multiplying the serendipitous events of the new generations. I confess that I always travel without a suitcase and do you know why? Because I never use anything twice and yet I never throw anything away. I maintain a constant necessity for the new and therefore I change name, I change reality, I change worlds, I change life, I change language, I change cultures, I change change, I change gear and continue onwards like one who does not care to go anywhere else. Esteemed Secretary of State, I ask you to lead this country in such a way as to avoid linear History. The influence we may exert over the world can cause repercussions in unexplored ways. We are all proof of the existence of celestial mechanics, we are all the said *black swan*. Our knowledge has its limits. And therefore, what we don't know is more relevant than what we do know. Be, for this nation, its third body.[7] And thus make the difference, by interfering, in a minuscule way, in society. Be that tiny disturbance in the system, which produces a radical change. And be fast! The massive presence of the image in our society is now inevitable following the invention of chromolithography. The image is all around us. Even if you close your eyes it is still there, fixed in your subconscious,[8] like a photograph. The scrapbook is no longer a 'grave' for locks of hair, or pressed flowers, but a box of dreams, abstractions of the spirit. I awake early and note down with care all the places I visit while I am asleep. In time I have become a capable manipulator of my inner world and I organize small philosophical reflections to read before going to sleep, which lead me to particular countries in my thinking.[9]

Estate AN/0007

Letter to Minister and Secretary of State João Franco, Rudolstadt, 27th of October 1899

Esteemed Minister and Secretary of State João Franco,

I hereby humbly present to you my plans for the implementation of an innovative method of workers' education in Portugal. I have been a builder of games for children and adults since 1885 for Richter & Co and author of science fiction novels, these being the forms I personally chose, to reach modernity. The kindergarten programme of the Froebel Institute is based on the principle of separating drawing from its artistic objective so it may be given to children. J.-J. Rousseau himself declared that to draw is to promote the coordination of the hand and the eye, thus considering it as a fundamental tool for the development of quality in workers and craftsmen. I believe that Art and Science can produce fundamental changes in society and that we can, through a specific type of education, construct a space in which pioneering artists and scientists may meet and join one another to change the century. In relation to what this education can be (and indeed already is) may I remind you that little by little optical illusion tents are becoming more and more popular throughout Europe, thus performing a precious and indirect role in social education and in the revolution of ideas. Oh, if politics was only brave enough, in the form of your good self, to ally itself to art and science in this desire to dominate the abstract. Your declared and official enthusiasm for the next Universal Exhibition shows that the union is possible, and I take the opportunity of informing you that I shall be publicly unveiling my first machine for seeing and feeling in four dimensions, dedicated to David Brewster.[10] In this prototype the visitor enters and holds a pair of binoculars whilst leaning against a moving wall, heated by salt crystals, which inclines until reaching the horizontal. The visitor loses his sense of gravity, because his feet are in the air, and his sense of space, because he gazes at an infinite horizon that is not there, where many birds fly over a long period of time. The mechanical eye of the image descends until we see a reclining man, smoking on a sandy beach (while this is happening

I smoke my melon-flavoured cigarillos into a metal fan which blows the smoke into the 4D-machine). A woman goes past (it is impossible to tell what or who she is) and at this precise moment I cast an unforgettable perfume into the machine and each of the visitors imagines his or her muse, without being burdened with the inconvenience of being obliged to see him or her as in my own image. This moment has the necessary momentum for one to imagine and then immediately a train passes, but this is also hardly seen, because what I show you is the equivalent of two frames of a train and the cacophony which I create with my sound machines deafens the ear of the visitor and startles those who await outside, creating a brief and marvellous sense of suspense, which leaves no clues, but goes well with the taste of the tea. Alva[11] shakes the moving wall and Chladni[12] is behind it with a capturemeter, attempting to register the sound of the visitor's breathing and transforming his cardiac rhythm into sound waves. The pencil moved by the energy of the sound waves produces a graphic curve in the form of a bird. When it seems like we are about to see what we cannot see, everything stops. We remove the binoculars, shine much light on his or her face and record the first impressions.

Estate AN/111

5th Excerpt of the 2010 Manifesto by Acácio Nobre:
'...I proclaim the end of the image (in 1910 or in 2010?) ... Art exists in us and happens to us, it cannot be archived.'

Estate AN/112

Acácio quotes Archimedes in his notebook:
'The slowness of my writing is my instrument for slowing down the world.'

Estate AN/35/65/9999

According to PIDE records, Acácio was not always Acácio. He was also called Fritz, Eduard Said, Antero Q., Naussibaum and Eduard Bey. The name Acácio Nobre appears between 1890 and 1945, a period during which he fled Portugal, was imprisoned in Spain, disappeared in Germany, was declared dead in Baku, reappeared in Belgium, was spotted in Paris and locked up in Amsterdam in an asylum where he socialized with Vincent Van Gogh's sister.

Estate AN/11/b

Letter on the NY Hotel notepaper dated Paris 16th of December 1923

No address, possible rough version for retrospective diary Paris 1916

Dear Alva,

I received the news of the death of another modernist poet with great sadness. All of my friends commit suicide, live clandestine lives, change identity, are imprisoned, or simply disappear. and without anyone daring to even mention their names. If I can't write to anybody, then I am truly alone. I ask you to read my letters, not for love, nor because you miss me, nor for mere interest, but for compassion. You need not reply. As proof that you have read them, return the opened letters to the Brasileira Café, with the envelope torn and I will know that you read them at least as far as these instructions. You need not add a single word to mine in reply. It is enough to hear from you that I am heard.

Yours always,
AN

Estate AN/800

Lisbon, 14th of March 1913

Esteemed Secretary of State,

Currently all governments wishing to have a competitive market are sending teachers and academics to France and Germany to learn the method of drawing that they intend to adopt in the industrial training in their countries. Programmes for the teaching of drawing are analyzed as if they were matters of espionage. It is imperative to understand why some countries triumph in Design Exhibitions and others do not. In 1863, more than fifty years ago, Alavin presented a detailed study regarding the state of artistic education in Belgium since 1850, listing the reasons for the failure of Belgian industrial products in the Universal Exhibitions of 1855 and 1862 in London, and comparing Belgian training to French training. Less than half a century later, profound changes in their educational system mean that today Belgium is on the very front line of industrial textiles and fashion, competing with the major European powers. I refer to the Belgian example as it is a country significantly smaller than our own, not only in size, but also in textile tradition! I would be so bold as to say that I consider myself the ideal person to lead such an ambitious project in Portugal. Not only thanks to my experience as an inventor of games and observer at the Froebel Institute, recently formed in Berlin, but for having grown up and lived side by side with the textile industry thanks to my father, an Azorean fisherman who came to France in 1816, where he learned to draw and became a worker; and most of all to Chevreul,[13] a friend of my father's with whom I spent all the afternoons of my adolescence.[14] It is imperative that we embark on this globalization of teaching methods. The domestication and the everyday use of science through the unification of Machines and Nature is a necessity. We are galloping towards modernity in all its forms. Social renewal begins with education, so preached the French Revolution more than a hundred years ago. We cannot continue with a government that does not invest in the future. It was with Richter & Co that I began my research into the childhood of the avant-garde, collecting evidence of the presence of our toys in the homes of artists, which has proved most revealing in helping us to understand the past of many amazing innovations. At the present moment I am in the process of developing a family tree of art, whose main objective is to prove that if the world neither plays, nor fictionalizes, it does not evolve.

Estate No 222/3333/444

I found the following note in the chest, from my grandmother, addressed to me: 'The sum of all the parts is not equal to a single person.'

Berlin, 5th of February 1908

Esteemed Minister and Secretary of State and Guardian of the Crown Portfolio, João Franco,

I recently met with the Baroness Bertha Von Marenholtz-Bülow in Vienna, and together we developed a plan for the progressive introduction of the kindergarten in Portugal, in order to create innovative foundations for future generations. The world can be fitted in a toy box exactly because it does not fit into any other place. You ask me: 'How do we make drawing accessible to all?' And I reply as Pestalozzi would have replied: 'By counting, measuring, and talking.' Only the latter of these would I change to 'thinking'. It is not necessary to talk to reach knowledge.

Baku, 6th of April 1909

My Dear and Esteemed Secretary of State,

To make a puzzle is to take a mental plunge into a game manipulated by the hands. I write to you again to introduce to you the 1st Plan of Mechanical Gymnastics for Future Industrial Workers. You will notice that the exercises become progressively difficult until the student has such a command over his hand of what his eye sees that he may draw from his mind, seeing and imagining invisible shapes that float before his eyes! The power of the imagination, esteemed Secretary of State. The power to re-create what is not there! Or indeed, is all that we can see truly within our grasp? Is everything real? I must confess that I spent a large part of my life confined to the 75cm of the top of my drawing table, writing and resolving mathematical equations and cosmological reflections, illustrating the elliptical orbits of celestial bodies. I have distanced myself more and more from reality and I feel no need whatsoever to return. Nor would I know where that is. Why return to a place we have perhaps never been? Well, as I said: when a student is able to represent all the shapes that I suggest in my appendix, he is ready to represent all of Nature and to be an excellent worker. And this is it! Knowledge is in the transaction of knowledge. And art is its first translator. Everything is the product of the spirit of its times, nothing is the result of the thoughts of a single man. What would become of the world if man believed in a preconceived and immutable society? If he did not dare or wish to change? It is the duty of every man to embrace his times in order to free himself of them. The air that we breathe is the same that Archimedes, Euclid, Leonardo, or Pessoa breathed. The air and the breath of the Universe that unwittingly made us, as Lao-Tze would say. The beginning of the transformation of shapes. Only beyond life exists that which makes life life, only beyond sound what makes sound sound and only beyond the image, what makes the image image. We cannot photograph it. Or rather, we can, but the image can never be fixed there, on the paper, on that which claims to never change. Archives are dispensable and serve only to invent History, not to tell it. The only necessary archive is that of the transformation of ideas. How are they born? Where do they come from? Art is our need for abstraction, our fascination with the invisible, and therefore the motor for the transformation of the visible. Hélas! The union of the known and the unknown through drawing! I am at your service and available to travel to Lisbon to discuss with you in person and in detail the plans for the implementation of the kindergarten in Portugal.

With grateful thanks for your attention regarding this project,

Yours cordially,
Acácio Nobre.

Estate AN/13

Plans for the drawing up of a family tree for Art, 1954

The avant-garde seen through the childhood of its creators:[15]

Estate AN/14

Three packets of a medicine later popularized as Fentanyl.

Acácio Nobre suffered from horrible pains, which he treated with this synthetic opiate, a powerful painkiller almost a hundred times stronger than morphine, with effect over a short period of time, but producing immediate relief; also reported as a cause of aphasia, amongst other disorders.[16]

Estate AN/27

Letter to Marinetti[17]

Manhufe 23rd of May 1929

Esteemed Mr Marinetti,

The reconciliation of Futurism with the love for the past is unacceptable. You meet once again, this time in Venice, surrounded by palaces, moonlight, libraries, and antique shops, everything that you have always despised. The many faces of contradiction. Really, time can do anything! The years have passed and I still ask myself: Death to Dantas,[18] why? Death to Marinetti. Is Marinetti already dead? Death to Marinetti's manifesto. And what if the manifesto is already dead? Death to death! And here we have a problem: eternity does not exist except in Art, which rises above all terrestrial laws. Art is quantum physics! But how can you understand this if a futurist cannot even plant a garden? Nor make calculations! Yes, because a futurist likes numbers, but understands nothing of mathematics, a futurist knows not even how to look at a painting! He loses himself. How can you love speed and not even have time to have time? Because a futurist does not understand that it is time that travels in us and not us that travel in time. You my dear retro-futurist, got stuck in some neurotic nationalism! Art has always taken politics much more seriously than politics takes itself, but you my dear fool, you sold it to those in power. Worse still: to the generals! You need inequality to guarantee you a permanent battle! You are stupid! War is the cleansing of the world? Well I tell you that it's ideas that kill. Yours, but also mine. We may all disappear in the centrifugal blink of an eye, but I would prefer rather to eat myself. I would still die for ideas, but they would be my own![19]

Yours sincerely,
Nobre.

Estate AN/23-5-8769

First notes on his retrospective diary, on sketch and grocery shop paper.

Retrospective Diary page 1

I decide to start writing a diary in rewind–by writing backwards I can face up to my times. Man can, in theory, escape all of the catastrophes of his century, thus maintaining himself free to think of a better future, free from the presumptions of the present. We do not all need to be held hostage by our collective past. I am sheltered by some Belgian nuns who live in silence in a convent in Brecht. I survived World War I without knowing of its existence and discover that words are only important to me for writing, not for speaking, only to turn reflections and thoughts visible. I abandon my speaking machine. I recycle all of its pieces to construct a writing machine that will accompany me to the end of my days. My stay in the convent was a long one, dressed as a nun, performing my daily tasks by day and dealing with my other me by night. My silence ended when Alva barged into the convent, not only shouting, but swearing. Her tone was so insulting that all the sisters took refuge in the convent bunker as if the Great War was not yet over. We managed to maintain the deafening volume of our voices until we were driven out by the nuns, horrified, convinced that I was an impostor, that I spoke after all, that I had a lover after all, that I was not fleeing a great war after all, that I was not a victim after all, after all, after all, after all. Everything could have been something else.

Estate AN/23

Acácio Nobre receives a telegram in reply to his letter to the Secretary of State

Dear sir

— Content of letter suspect.
— Possible espionage.
— Present yourself on 24th,
  at Rua António Maria Cardoso, Nº 18.
— No other business.

From Secretary of State

And immediately afterwards, attached to the above, a non-official telegram:

Dear Nobre,

— Too early for reply.
— Country not know how to read let alone draw.
— Forget it.
— Leave country.
— Your admirer,
— (Call me Oliveira)[20]

Alva and heart failures

I met Alva when she was 82 years old. She had used a corset all her life and had recently been operated on to put her organs back into the correct order. As they had all moved upwards, they were the cause of various ailments, as well as considerable difficulty in eating and sitting. I had hardly entered when she said:

— The only thing that is truly important in a couple is sex. We spent a whole afternoon talking about Acácio.
— The two of us rarely appeared together in public: Acácio never spoke, I talked shit! Alva was incredibly beautiful, slim, seductive, but as she suffered from Tourette's syndrome, she cursed constantly!
— 'To choose to have time is to choose to not be part of this world' was the last note he left on my kitchen table. I knew I would never see him again.

The two of us contemplated Acácio's jewel, the famous purveyor of feminine pleasures, which dominated the gossip and conversations of the womenfolk of the French Surrealist circuit. I gaze at this bringer of joy, this catalyst of the clitoris, and Alva tells me that Acácio kept a private collection of photographs of the smiles of the users of the jewel. She places the jewel in my hand.

Do you want it? Take it.

After having asked for a detailed examination of the jewel by a forensic expert I discovered it seemed it had never been used.

In April 1974, Acácio asked Alva if she could help him to come back to Portugal to see the Revolution. It was the first time he flew.

Upon arriving in Lisbon, he went straight to an anti-PIDE demonstration and was hit by a bullet. In the testicles. He died, according to hospital records, as a result of cardiac arrest, just as a famous Portuguese poet did, on the morning of the Carnation Revolution, in the Largo do Carmo.

But don't we all die because our heart stops?

At his funeral, the twenty acquaintances in attendance (none of them family) all brought a book, all wore a bow tie and all sat drinking masala chai, eating rich tea biscuits with butter, and writing, celebrating the great man that was Acácio Nobre.

His epitaph reads: 'Everything could have been something else.'[21]

Patrícia Portela

Excerpts from the script of The Private Collection of Acácio Nobre performed in Performatik 2011 at Kaaitheater studios.

The translation of this text into English was done by Patrícia Portela and is a fragment of the book *The Private Collection of Acácio Nobre*, published by Caminho Publishing House in 2016.

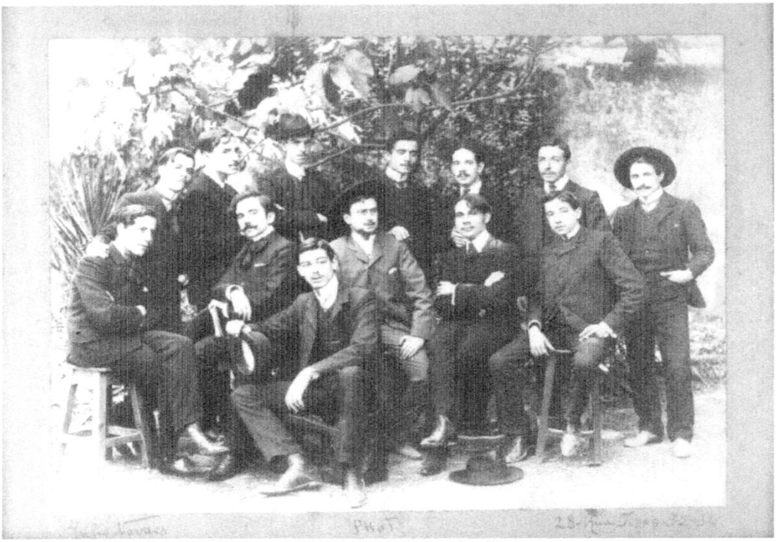

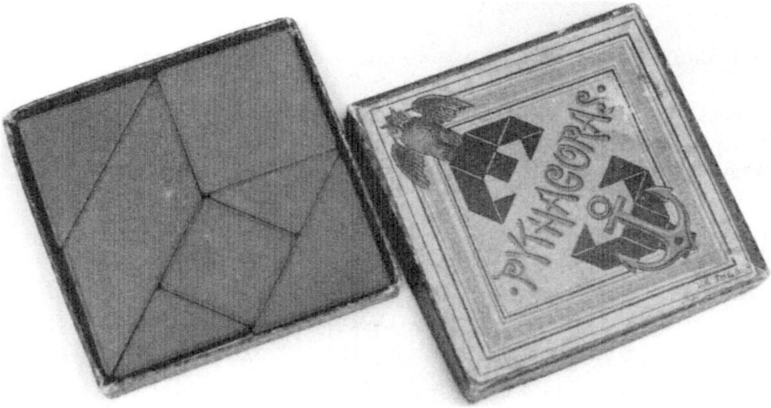
·PYTHAGORAS·

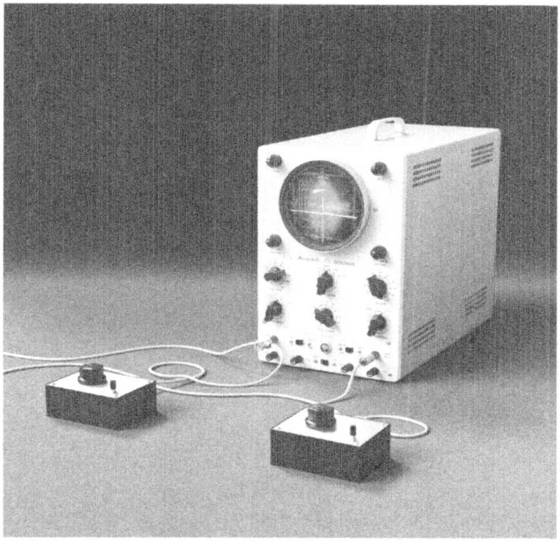

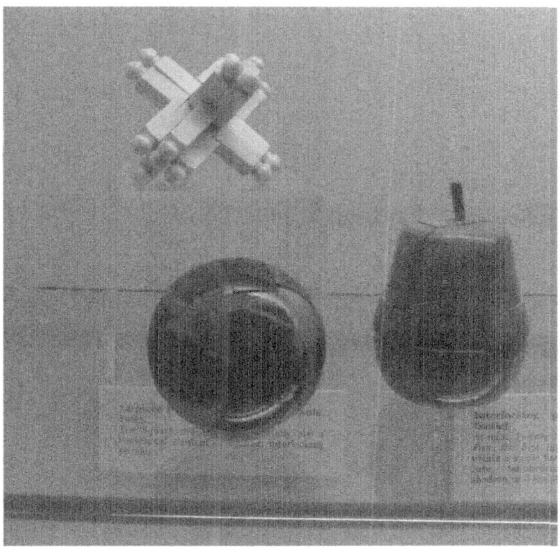

Paris, 30 de Abril de 1916

Cherida Alva,

Recebi a nothycia da morthe dhe maiz um poetha modhernistha com thristhezA. Thodhos os meus amigos se suicydham, vivem clandhesthinamenthe, mudham dhe idhenthidhadhe, são prezos, ou simplesmenthe dhezaparecem sem che ninguém se athreva a falar sobre elles. Si não posso escrever a alguém, então esthou verdhadheiramenthe sozinho. Peço-lhe che leia as minhas carthas, já não por amor, nem por saudhadhe, nem por mero inthéresse, mas por compaixão.

Não precisa dhe rethribuir.

Como prova dhe sua leithura, dhevolva estha cartha aberta n'A Brazileira, com o envelope rasgadho, e saberei que a leu pelo menos até estas insthruções.

Não precisa dhe acrescenthar às minhas pallavras uma única dhe volta. Bastha-me saber dhe se che sou ouvidho.

Sempre seu

A. N.

645 FATIMA P 311TJ LISBOA F

Linha ou mesa n.º

Estação

Entendido às

Por

Marca do dia

72

Número local	Categoria	Destino	Origem	Número origem	Palavras	Data	Hora
L8159		CHIADO LISBOA	831 42 12 1200				

MUI NOBRE SR., É MUITO CEDO PARA RESPOSTA. PAÍS NÃO SABE LER,
MUITO MENOS DESENHAR.DEIXE-SE DISSO. SAIA DO PAÍS.
CORDIAIS CUMPRIMENTOS,

(TRATE-ME POR OLIVEIRA)+

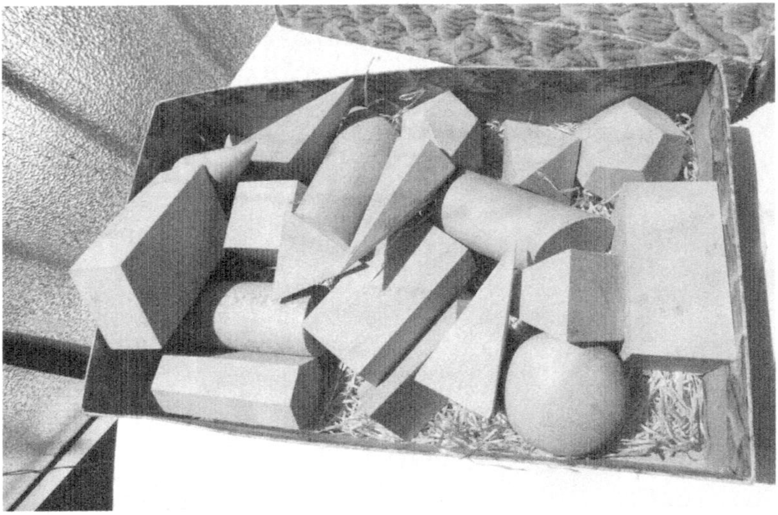

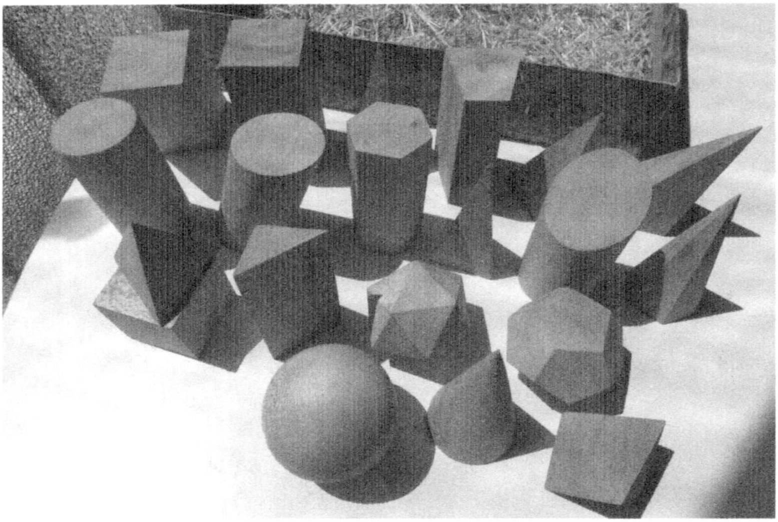

Rudolstadt, 7 de julho de 1891

Exchellenthyssimo Senhor
Ministhro e Secrethário d'Esthado dhos Negócyos dha
Insthrução Pública e Bellas Arthes
João Franco

Escrevo-lhe sobre o meu projecto de consolidhação do Insthithutho Fröbel no nosso pays. Por thodha a Europa é crescente a vonthade dhe muytos pedhagogos thornarem o esthudo dho dhezenho acessyvel a thodhos e não apenas a arthistas e a aristhocrathas abasthadhos. Para che o dhezenho posse chegar às mãos dhe thodos os che prethendam occupar o se thempo com o andamentho da socyedade, novas convenções dho dhezenho tem sido estudhadhas e ensayadhas athé à exaustão. É incontornável o exchellenthe effeito che a simpliffição dha Nathureza através dha Geomethria tem no dhesenvolvimentho dhas mayores pothências mundhiais. E porché? Porche um bom operário é achele que them uma boa vizão, e os princypios da vizão insthinthyva são: primeiro, a linha rectha; dhepois, o chuadhradho. A partir dhas subdhivisões dhe um chuadhradho, thodhas as fformas são possíveis. E a dhivizão dhe um chuadhradho é a multiplicação do thriângulo. E o segredo dha modernidhadhe está na sua nova representhação plana e na rendhoção dhos sólidhos dhe Plathão. Chuando um homem souber dezenhar um cone, um cubo e uma esffera na perffeição, conhece

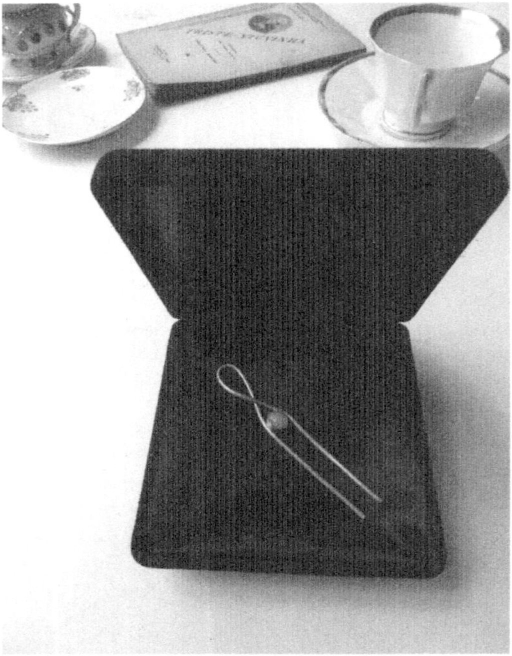

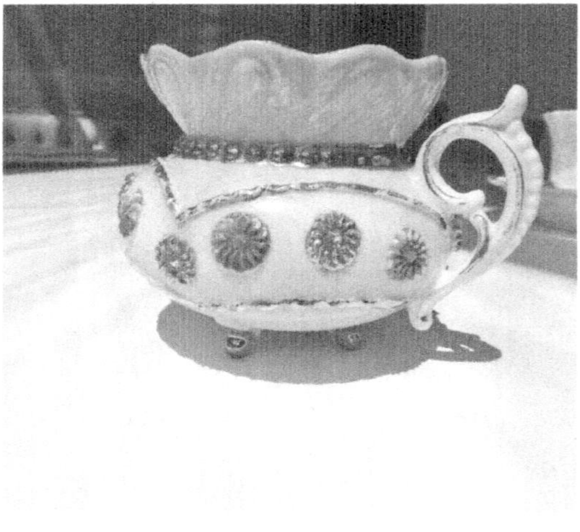

Images

- Estate An/0002-1928 group photo present in attachment of the portuguese secret police file 453/07 from 1939 of the geometric operation. In this photo, about which Centro Nacional de Cultura kindly gaves some information, we can see José Pacheko (1885-1934), The 'relatively famous architect' on the right, with a hat at his feet, and we suspect but are not sure that amongst this group modernist painter Eduardo Viana, seated on a bench on the left side, hugging, who knows? Perhaps artist Santa-Rita, ahead of Raul Lino, architect and writer with his forever hairy moustache, standing, next to Franco, Manuel Jardim, Acácio Lino, João Quintinha and perhaps Acácio Nobre. If so, this will be the only photo we have of him.
- Estate AN/4 - Tangram by Richter & Co
- Estate AN/5 - Plan Nr 44/08 Volleyscope
- Estate AN/6 - Ovoid puzzle exposed at the Indianapolis Museum of Art, USA, photograph by Patrícia Portela
- Estate AN/11/b - Letter to Alva, Paris 1916
- Estate AN/23 - Telegram to dictator Oliveira Salazar
- Estate AN/0044 - Gift box with Froebel solids that belonged to Acácio Nobre, photograph by Patrícia Portela, private collection of Alva Ramalho
- Estate AN/345 - Letter to João Franco, Rudolstadt
- Estate AN/1001 - Pleasure enhancer, jewel designed by Alva Ramalho offered to Acácio Nobre, photograph by Patrícia Portela, private collection
- Image 4 - Tea cup that belonged to Acácio Nobre and that used to belong to the French café Les Deux Magots, photograph by Patrícia Portela

Notes

1 Handwritten note found in the chest. The handwriting seems similar to that of my grandfather but the accents look like mine.

2 João Franco was a central political figure in Portugal for several decades, becoming famous for attacking the monarchist parties, forming coalitions with them, proclaiming himself a liberal, a conservative, a monarchist dictator or a Republican Party supporter, according to the flavour of the time. He managed to be hated by all resolving the situation by requesting the King to forbid any form of opposition to his rule. The monarchy turned its back on him too late. On the 6th of October 1910 a journalist wrote: 'After a long struggle, the monarchy itself implanted the Republic in Portugal.'

3 The document ends here.

4 This game was launched at the same International Meeting of Puzzle Makers in Florence where Nobre had, some years earlier, launched his greatest success, the Ovoid Puzzle. This time, however, the electronic game, despite its brilliance, never went on sale. Weighing 85kg, it was very difficult to transport and was financially unviable. The rejection of this new toy marked the beginning of Acácio's decline. 38 years later William Higinbotham launched a very similar tennis game, today officially recognized as the precursor of all computer games.

5 The document ends here.

6 At the end of the 19th century Europe was divided between those countries that embraced the study of drawing and unwittingly invented modernity based on the most basic laws of competitiveness, and other governments who forbade the kindergarten for fear of free thought. The industrial revolution paved the way for a simplification of the geometry of the body and for the study of colour through patterns and contrasts. The breakaway from existing educational models was the moment the avant-garde began.

7 Henri Poincaré was an aristocratic 19th-century mathematician who did not correct the spelling mistakes of his texts as he considered this to be a waste of time. He rewrote the Theory of the Third Body, which later formed the basis of the Chaos Theory. This superstar of theories was popularized by the famous image of the butterfly that beats its wings in America causing a hurricane in Japan.

8 It should be pointed out that the theories of the subconscious were at this time very recent and absolutely revolutionary and fashionable.

9 The theory of the Black Swan. All swans are white until a single black swan proves the theory wrong. Everything is (or seems) as it is until proven otherwise.

10 Acácio Nobre was born on the day and in the year of the death of David Brewster, the man of the first stereoscope, who polarized light and invented the kaleidoscope.

11 Alva was the woman who gave Acácio the famous jewel that he always carried in his pocket, attached to a watch chain. 'It is useful for passing the time well, rather than checking what the time is', Acácio would comment about this jewel, with no little irony. I always thought Alva held the key to my understanding of Acácio and I pursued any records of her life I could find for years and years.

12 When Acácio refers to Chladni, he actually refers to Chladni son. The father, Ernst Florenz Friedrich Chladni (1756–1827) was a German physicist and professor at Breslau. He published a treatise on acoustics that went on to influence the visual arts and was the first person to convert sound vibrations into drawings. He had two sons, one of whom was deaf and a great childhood friend of Acácio Nobre.

13 Chevreul, the renowned French chemist, was the director of the department of dyes at the carpet factory in Les Gobelins where Acácio's father also worked. Interested in improving the brightness of the colours, he came to the conclusion that their brightness was, irrespective of the chemical quality of the dye, caused by an optical illusion, the meeting between the eye and the colour. His theories indirectly influenced a whole generation of painters. 'To imitate a model, we must copy it in a way which is different to what we see', Chevreul would always tell Acácio.

14 A curiosity: Chevreul was also one of the forerunners of geriatrics, dying at the age of 102.

15 It was with Richter & Co that Acácio began his research into the childhood of the avant-garde, collecting evidence of toys produced by Richter & Co present in the homes of artists. His main objective was to prove that 'if the world neither plays, nor fictionalizes, it does not evolve'. Acácio Nobre believed that a Russian box containing eight wooden toys, on sale in the mid-nineteenth century, led Malevich to invent Modernism in the twentieth century, that *The Elements of Drawing* by Ruskin, published in 1857 had originated mainly of French Impressionism, that the first geometric puzzles by Richter & Co in 1880 inspired a young Kandinsky to invent abstraction between 1910 and 1913. An ethnographic collection is exhibited in Paris and two of its visitors spread cubism all over Europe. The Froebelian education of Frank Lloyd Wright brings us Modern and Organic Architecture.

A butterfly flaps its wings in Japan and...

The first black swan appears in Australia and...

16 Aphasia is a language disorder. Although people who suffer from it may be able to write or sing, sufferers may not be able to speak. Aphasia is the result of a brain lesion provoked by cardiac arrest or concussion. Symptoms include: excessive creativity in the use of personal neologisms; persistent repetition of the same sentences, or phrases, and incapacity to speak spontaneously.

On the rare occasions the sufferers manage to speak, they may often do so in palindromes–words and numbers that can be read both forwards and backwards–such as radar, civic, madam, level, or even sentences such as 'Was it a rat I saw?', 'Step on no pets', 'Madam, I'm Adam', 'You can cage a swallow, can't you, but you can't swallow a cage, can you?'. Artists who have suffered from this illness (although not necessarily expressing themselves through palindromes) include Malevich, Jonathan Swift, and Acácio Nobre.

17 The letter to Filippo Tommaso Emilio Marinetti was the reason the Portuguese Futurists distanced themselves from Acácio Nobre and from that day on refused even to mention his name.

18 Dantas was the director of the Fine Arts School in Lisbon who had refused a whole generation of modernist painters and was used in the futurist Manifesto as a symbol of Academism in Art.

19 The final paragraph of a letter to Marinetti refers directly to the Anthropophagic Movement that began in Brazil and which found, in Acácio, one of its greatest followers in Portugal and in Europe.

20 António de Oliveira Salazar was a dictator and the creator of the 'New State', greatly inspired by fascist ideologies. He perpetuated the idea of Portugal as a pluricontinental empire, being responsible for the killing of thousands of people in the colonial wars and supported a secret police that repressed all basic liberties and political freedom. Despite all of this, he was elected 'Greatest Portuguese Ever' in a tv contest two years after Father Damien was elected 'De Grootste Belg' for Flanders and Jacques Brel 'Le plus grand Belge' for the French-speaking part of Belgium.

21 The kindergarten of Froebel was never introduced in Portugal.

Part 2

Alternative Visions on the Present

The Fragile I
The Power and Vulnerability of Your Own Voice in Podcasts

Katharina Smets

When I tell a story, I am constructing a reality that is a reflection of how I experience it. I do this with my voice, the recordings I've made, and the scenario I've written based on my experiences. I can make rules for this reality. I can reduce the immense complexity of our chaotic, everyday reality to a few lines and follow the patterns I have set for myself. My person can be visible or concealed, but I will be there, regardless of how I tell the story. The choice for telling a story comprises the choice to express myself. When I also choose to tell the story in the first person, I am involving my vulnerable self in the game.

The personal essay, in which the world is reflected through the eyes of a first-person narrator, made its debut in the sixteenth century, introduced by the philosopher Michel de Montaigne, and since then has never really gone away. Even then this approach was hardly new, as more than a thousand years earlier Augustine of Hippo had shown with his Confessions that his profound self-scrutiny meant he had to throw himself into the fray. His autobiographical approach was essential for his theological and philosophical development. The first person is elastic, and appears to be able to adapt itself continuously to contemporary forms of literary and journalistic writing, films, or audio stories, whether fictional or documentary.

Often the first-person narrator in a documentary is rightly or wrongly regarded as, or held to be, identical to the author of the work. In the case of an audio work, it is after all usually the voice of the author, which blurs the distinction between author and narrator even more. The reasons why authors use the first person may differ and in the past few years I have switched over from creating documentary work in which I consistently removed myself, to being an autobiographical narrator; at least in part. The moment that I became visible as the narrator, other unanticipated narrative mechanisms came into effect. I became one of the players in a greater whole. I became an active character in my audio essays, so I began to see new ways of looking at reality, and the strategies I used to approach these then became part of my story. I describe these patterns and rules with reference to my own work and the work of storytellers whose work is dear to me.

I Am a Machine

'I am alienated from myself and transformed into an object, a remembering and formulating machine.'[1] The Austrian writer and dramatist Peter Handke writes these words in his account *A Sorrow Beyond Dreams* (*Wunschloses Unglück*) in which he tries to come to grips with the life and suicide of his mother. He wrote everything down in an attempt to place his emotions, in order to counter the 'dull speechlessness' that accompanied her death.

> When I write, I necessarily write about the past, about something which, at least while I am writing is behind me. As usual when engaged in literary work, I am alienated from myself and transformed into an object, a remembering and formulating machine. I am writing the story of my mother, first of all because I think I know more about her and how she came to her death than any outside investigator who might, with the help of a religious, psychological, or sociological guide to the interpretation of dreams, arrive at a facile explanation of this interesting case of suicide; but second in my own interest, because having something to do brings me back to life; and lastly because, like an outside investigator, though in a different way, I would like to represent this VOLUNTARY DEATH as an exemplary case.[2]

When Handke writes the story of his mother, he writes about his wish to make the events into a case. A case that is circumscribed, that has comprehensible patterns and can be understood. A case that exists outside of him, so that it no longer hurts as much.

> I look back on them as intermittent 'states': suddenly my day-to-day world–which after all, consists only of images repeated *ad nauseam* over a period of years and decades since they were new–fell apart, and my mind became so empty that it ached.[3]

In these first pages of his story Handke tells how he steps out of himself and becomes a machine, while at the same time he does not want to cede his story to 'any outside investigator', even though a more journalistic approach might be able to 'solve' the story more quickly in one way or another. As if it was a riddle, something that when looked at in the right way could chase away the horror vacui. It is precisely this struggle of the writer as son, author, deeply grieving man with insoluble questions that makes this narrative what it is. Fragments of daily reality are arranged in a search for identity and identification.

Because Handke exposes his personal struggle with reality so lucidly, I can use his thoughts to illustrate the fragility and the vulnerability of the author who chooses to narrate a personal story. The documentary art that I describe are audio stories that are made specifically for listening. They make use of editing, music, and narration, the various elements of the medium called radio. In these stories, which traditionally are called radio features, not every audio producer feels a need to use his or her own voice. Even so, they are always the expression of the internal world of the maker, a world that is subject to the author's personal rules of play.

I spoke to four makers, two men and two women from different countries and each with their own distinct traditions. Alan Hall is the founder of Falling Tree,[4] a London-based independent production house. It has been hailed as one of the leading production houses for artistic documentaries about historic, psychological, or cultural subjects. Hall trained as a composer, and the musicality of his documentaries is undeniable.

Rikke Houd is an independent producer who lives on a small island between Poland and Denmark. Over the past twenty years she has brought us exceptional work in five different languages: Danish, Swedish, Norwegian, Icelandic, and English. Hers are stories between reality and legend, in which the sea and inhospitable mountain landscapes of the high North always seem to play a part.

Jonathan Goldstein is a writer and radio producer from Brooklyn, NYC. In *WireTap*, the show he makes for Canadian radio, he brings us stories in which the distinction between reality and fiction blurs and his parents and friends are recurring actors. After eleven years he returned to the United States and now he has a new podcast called *Heavyweight*, in which he tries, for himself, friends and family to clear up the questions that keep them awake at night. Recently he has started taking on cases for strangers as well.

Finally, Kaitlin Prest started to make audio stories for *Audio Smut*, her sex show, which she used to produce in Montreal. In 2014, she founded *The Heart*, a podcast that brings stories about intimacy and humanity, documentary narratives that sometimes take a fictional turn.

All four storytellers make a form of documentary audio and have a pronounced personal style and voice, even if that voice is not always literally heard. These makers have had an influence on my work and after several years of listening to their stories, their voices and opinions have become familiar to me. Some of them have also become colleagues and friends. Like me, these makers do indeed sometimes use journalistic resources and interview techniques to bring themselves closer to a sort of authenticity, in contrast to Handke's narration. Maybe this is still an echo from the time that radio was used primarily as a news medium. As makers of audio stories we make use of what is available to us. The London-based media expert Tim Crook calls this 'the five dimensions of audio narrative', namely, the spoken word, music, sound, silence, and the imagination of the listener.[5] These are the means that give us, as makers, the ability to move as characters in our own stories, to become, in the words of Handke, the 'memory and formulating machine' that is necessary for setting the narrative mechanisms in motion.

I'm Not Here, But You Can Hear Me

Alan Hall never uses his voice as the narrator. In this connection he has said, 'In making documentary features, if I find I have to keep myself in or put myself in, it is a sign of failure. That was my established viewpoint, for a long, long time.'[6]

Alan Hall rings me up, while enjoying a cup of tea, from his small studio in a redbrick building in the heart of Blackheath-Village in South-East London.

'Why', I ask him. 'Katharina', he replies, 'I'm English, I'm shy. I'm diffident, it's part of our DNA. Heavens above, no really, me? No. It's not... it just doesn't feel natural.' Alan says that talking about himself makes him feel extremely uncomfortable. I can hear that in his voice, while he marshals his arguments. 'Also, I'm not a talker when I don't feel like I have anything to say, whereas the people I talk to, now they have something to say. Why would I get in the way, why don't I just let them speak?'

Alan Hall makes intimate, musical radio documentaries for BBC Radio 3, Radio 4 and the World Service, among others. Although his voice itself is not to be heard, his style is unmistakeable. An important aspect of his features is his respect for and the space he gives to the people he interviews. It's as if you as listener were actually talking to the interviewee yourself, without the filter of a narrator.

> I'm not judging anyone else doing it. Some other people are brilliant and they do have things to say. And they have a particular tone of voice or they have an ability to reflect and digest and reproduce ideas that I don't necessarily think I have.

Some of Alan's radio documentaries have a political slant. He does not see himself as a maker of programmes in which he intrudes, rather he sees his role as that of somebody who helps others tell their stories. His choice for not making use of a narrator is, in the context of the BBC, almost an act of rebellion. He gives a voice to people and groups that one rarely hears on BBC's Radio 4, unless they have become a talking point. In his stories he reverses the roles, placing the interviewee in the role of narrator in order to show us around worlds and communities that are relatively inaccessible to the middle-class and largely white listener. It's a matter of contact between the narrators and their contact with the listener. Alan has the ability to win the confidence of his narrators, to make himself virtually invisible, and subsequently, in the editing stage, to make it into an aesthetically pleasing document. 'It is not about me, although obviously I'm in there, my fingerprints are all over everything. It's not about me, it is about the relationship between the story, the storyteller, the production, and the listener.'

To this day, Alan Hall's documentaries are an example to me. His attention to the narrators and their stories, the musicality and painstaking editing that raises the interviews and scenes to the level of gems of documentary art. I too felt it was unsuitable, for reasons of respect for the storytellers and the story, to insert myself between them and the listener. Even so I was already there. My particular questions, interviewing technique, and recording methods, and the direction of the location in which the interview was recorded. I deliberately manoeuvred the storytellers into places that would evoke memories, I referred to photographs from the past, and asked them to interact with people in their surroundings. These are techniques I had learned from Alan. Recently, Alan has somewhat revised his opinion. The immediate cause was a documentary he made about the American singer Elly Stone. He had interviewed her in the studio and shared a cab with her on the way to a café, all the while recording as much as he could, as Alan's time with the singer was only limited. Once back in his hotel room, he felt he had completely blown the interview. He would have to let himself be heard in the story. In the documentary, I heard Alan telling Elly Stone how the interview would proceed, what distance he would hold the microphone away from her to ensure that her voice sounded warm. He is moved when she sings for him, a side of himself he seldom shows.

> Because it gave me an authority, it wasn't just found material. It was my material. And the reason why the person was speaking the way they were speaking was because I had been talking to them and I had recorded them. So, sometimes the modest English need to overcome their reticence and perhaps accept that they do have individual qualities that can be of benefit to programmes.

It was at Alan Hall's production house that I learned about the work of the Danish producer Rikke Houd.[7] I heard the delicate voice of a woman, intimate yet respectfully distant. Stories recorded in landscapes of ice, with ink-black birds in the sky, and voices that are rarely granted a forum: refugees, the homeless, Inuit from Greenland and Canada, a singing soothsayer from Iceland. A couple of years later, in the here and now, Rikke and I have become friends. We regularly chat about audio and the challenges of our profession. Although she has been making audio stories for twenty years now, in the first ten years she used to cut her voice out of her pieces. Slowly she began to move in her pieces as an interviewer, until she was the narrator.

> An 'I' can be so many things in a radio feature, just like the 'I' of a novel or a poem. It's a tricky balance, introducing an 'I' into an audio story. It can elevate a story and ruin it too. It took me out of my comfort zone the first time I did it, mainly because I didn´t feel like drawing attention to me. I think the first significant 'audio-I' I heard was in the work of Swedish Lotta Eriksson. Personal, humoristic and political.

In addition, in the Danish broadcasting tradition it was unusual to use the I form.

'But then I made a story with a cryptic I, and I used very few details. It was a lyrical I that could set the borders of the story, I felt. But not so much that it became realistic.' Rikke quotes an old fable to clarify what she means. A woman goes to the market, but she may not be dressed and nor may she be nude, she may not walk on the road and nor may she walk in the fields. 'I often think about that fable and that image when I work.' Eventually the woman dons a fishnet and walks on the verge. 'Realism on one side, and poetry on the other.'

I ask her if there are dangers lurking in her method. She tells me that when she is recording, she feels like she is entering a slightly altered universe, hyperreal and poetic or mythical at the same time. Because she works with real stories about real people, she thinks it very important to reproduce the reality accurately, albeit with a filter. The danger can lie in adding a mythological layer relating to the poetry of a story, but which is nonetheless not true to the person or event that she is describing. Rikke is constantly asking herself if the person she is representing would be satisfied with the image she is creating. Or if she sees them better through the patterns she starts to see.

What Rikke describes, I encounter again in the words of Bill Nichols, an American film critic, and pioneer of documentary film theory:

> The voice of an orator, or documentarian, enlists and reveals desires, lacks, and longings. It charts a path through the stuff of the world that gives body to dreams and substance to principles. Speaking, giving voice to a view of the world, makes possible the necessary conditions of visibility to see things anew, to see, as if for the first time, what had, until now, escaped notice. This is not objective sight but seeing in that precarious, fleeting moment of insight when a gestalt clicks into place and meaning arises from what had seemed to lack it or to be already filled to capacity with all the meaning it could bear.[8]

A number of years ago I was wandering about, lost, in Paris. It seems to be part of a fixed pattern when making stories: that they only come into being when I'm free of familiar surroundings and can see and hear what is happening around me. I had just visited La Maison de la Radio (House of the Radio), and full of admiration I had inspected the studios where they still made radio plays. The gravel in boxes, the tape on the ground to imitate the sound of fallen leaves. When I was sitting at a table in the France Culture radio studio, a passing producer asked if I was the actress who was to read the Tolkien texts.

'No', said I, 'Unfortunately not.'

I first have to get lost to find a story before I can read it out, I thought to myself. In the final pages of his novella *A Sorrow Beyond Dreams*, between the short anecdotes and rather everyday memories he has of his mother, Peter Handke writes: 'Sometimes, of course, as I worked on my story, my frankness and honesty weighed on me and I longed to write something that would allow me to dissemble a bit, a play, for instance.'[9]

It was a grey day in Paris, and the area I found myself in was banal. Upriver stood the Eiffel tower, a few tourist boats turned around here so that they could return to the more interesting parts of the city. With my back to the large building of Radio France, I decided to walk over the Pont de Grenelle, towards the small version of the Statue of Liberty in the middle of the bridge. The statue stands on a long thin island, in the middle of the Seine. When I got there, I saw that somebody had painted small white dots on the statue's base. The dots continued along the wall under the bridge and led to a plastic tent. Around the tent somebody had made a garden and in front of the tent a woman was sitting, calmly doing her laundry. Every now and then she would stand up and lower a bucket into the Seine to get more water. The bucket was also dappled with white spots. I took out my recorder from my bag and pressed record. This was the start of the audio story *Senza Parole*[10] that I made about the woman under the bridge, about the conversations I tried to have with her, and eventually a song that turned out to be the only connection between us: an Italian tear-jerker about a couple who no longer understand each other.

The evening before this meeting, the Dutch writer Adriaan van Dis had impressed on me that when he wrote a documentary, he tried to return at least three times to the place or the person about whom he was writing, because your experience can change or acquire greater depth. Because you yourself change, I think. Every time I go back to Liliana under the bridge, I tell myself to bring a question, or an object. It is a way of directing myself, of setting a possible scene in motion. I had also told myself to use my own voice for the first time and a first-person narrator, to weave a stream of consciousness into the sound of reality. My self-imposed rules forced me to be in the moment with the listener, to make the scene happen in the here and now. To keep the experience as authentic as possible I refrained from filtering out my own doubts, nervous laughs, and unease as much as possible. My overdubbed narrative voice could not clarify, only show. I was a woman clad in a fishnet, somewhat embarrassed by my nakedness, with one foot in the lyrical and the other foot in reality.

I Am Not God

Regardless of how close or far the I stands in the art of the maker, it will always be a stylized I. The paradox is that by adopting such artifices the I-narrator creates a more 'authentic' effect; as if it was all such a spur-of-the-moment idea and conversation, without any filters or direction. The Dutch author Connie Palmen, known for her largely autobiographical novels, describes her first-person narrator as 'not an acted character, but rather a restrained character– a controlled brand, a controlled image'.[11]

As the narrator in my autobiographical audio stories I direct myself to the extent that I decide just how confused, nervous, clever, or sometimes stupid I sound, just for the authenticity effect. Paradoxically, audio work often requires long training in speaking and writing in order to make the voice sound credible: hours, days, years in my case.

The same applies to Ira Glass, the producer and host of an extremely popular radio show called *This American Life*, and an example for many a teller of audio stories. 'When I was learning to do it, I would take and retake and retake, and then I would edit it to death to get it to sound natural.'

The paradox that Ira Glass talks about, is very recognizable. 'Essentially, for you to perform a version of yourself on the air, you're having to learn the craft of actually being an actor.'[12]

In short, as a radio maker you are often both actor and producer. When I, as maker, am recording an interview for a documentary scene or out recording in the world, there is always an internal producer listening in–an internal producer who is watching over my managed image, to make sure that the dramaturgy of the desired storyline is respected and to ensure that the dramatic arc of the scene remains taut. The producer imposes the filter on the reality so that I can see the links and draw a narrative thread out of the chaos. The internal producer also watches over the extent to which I must reveal my real, everyday human self in the story to ensure that it remains credible.

Unlike Alan Hall or Rikke Houd, Jonathan Goldstein has never worked as a journalist. His audio stories are the result of his work as a writer and comedian, where the first person was the natural approach. The use of the first person in literature is associated with a code that we know better, an I that makes a connection between an internal world and an external reality. In Goldstein's new podcast, *Heavyweight*, the maker chooses for the external reality, although his I narrator is highly lyrically stylized.

> I always thought that starting with I was an open acknowledgement of something that both I and the audience already know: that the broadcast isn't coming from some kind of omniscient gas. That there is a person who is telling them a story.

Recently the first-person narrator in Jonathan's stories has come closer to his autobiographical self. Through his interactions with his wife, his best friends, and radio colleagues, you get the feeling that you are really starting to know a person:

> Hopefully the acknowledgement of this makes the following feel more genuine and authentic and can also have a disarming kind of quality to it and activate that part of a listener's brain that they reserve for hearing stories from their friends.

Jonathan springs forth from a literary tradition. Unencumbered by a past of objective reporting he has always staked his I as a narrator and freely refined it. More than Alan and even more than Rikke, Jonathan tries to reveal himself so that he can touch the listener. 'My aspiration [with the new series] is to try to get closer to the heart, and to allow myself to be a little bit more revealing and vulnerable.'

I Am a Vulnerable Story

'I feel like every time I make a story about myself it is only good when there is a part of it that is really painful', says Kaitlin Prest. 'And really sad. So every time I make a personal story, there is a part of it that hurts so much.'

To take the metaphor of the fable referred to by Rikke Houd one step further, Kaitlin would be standing naked in the middle of the road, just to see what happens. Kaitlin started making radio because of her social commitment, her desire to give marginalized groups a voice. In Canada these are often themes that are associated with race and indigenous peoples and after a while Kaitlin as a white became uneasy about giving their stories shape and editing their truth. She herself belonged more to the queer and transgender community, and so she started with her *Audio Smut* sex show. Her decision to use the I-form had also to do with logistics.

> There were a lot of times when I was working on the sex show, and it was difficult to find somebody who was willing to go into the detail or the depth, or the discomfort that was required to make a good honest piece about sexuality.

For Kaitlin the solution was plain:

> I had a really clear ethical and creative imperative of why it was important. And I believed in it. So, it was much easier to put myself in that vulnerable position than to ask other people to do it. Because I already dedicated my life to doing that.

For her it is less of a risk to stake herself than others. Kaitlin is not afraid of appearing to be stupid, ugly, or bad in her stories. She makes her masturbation, heartaches, and loves into artistic documentaries.

In her recent series entitled *No,*[13] about consent and borderlines in sex, she goes one step further. Taking a story from her personal archive she lets the listener hear how she had sex with somebody, although she had clearly said 'no' earlier on. She then visits her friend Jay, to ask him why he insisted on masturbating together, even though she clearly did not want to. In this respect Kaitlin shows how reducing the entire reality to a narrative tale can damage the story. 'Because you need this tidy beginning middle and end, and a clear conflict. There is some real damage that can be done in choosing narrative to represent life. Especially when it comes to something really fraught.'

> My friend Jay is the plot point who got reduced to something smaller than his whole person in service of the narrative.

> I framed it in such a way, that this assholeness of his was highlighted. He became a very one-dimensional character in that story, and nobody is one-dimensional.

As listener I have the impression that it's Jay himself who was mainly responsible for this. Although at the same I can, in connection with *Writer*, feel guilty about how I portrayed the author, even though it was, in this case too, the man himself who was entirely responsible for it, as will become apparent below. I recognize my own feelings in Kaitlin, when she says, 'I would rather fuck up my own relationships and my own life, than do a story about someone else and fuck up their relationships and their life.'

As an audio story maker, I do not always have external reality under control. While I walk through the world with my recorder, I try to record the world as it is, but at the same time I try to contain it in the structure and patterns that make the story complete. The arbitrary, chaotic reality is, however, not a play that I can turn into a logically structured story, as Peter Handke complained. Reality takes no directions, and that ultimately makes the story into a documentary rather than a fictional feature. What I can do though, is to try and recognize patterns that give structure to reality, so that the narrative line can become a story. I can direct myself. I have an internal producer who listens in while I'm recording documentary material, and who recognizes patterns in the story and tries to give direction to them. I can try to control the process by considering what I am saying during the recordings and my machine is running, or by how I describe the facts in voice-over afterwards. But as I have said, reality does not always cooperate. Sometimes, when you as first-person narrator are part of the story, you simply have to take part in the chaos. There are times when the I in the external world becomes all too painfully vulnerable. This, however, is the sine qua non if I as a narrator wish to give an honest picture of the chaotic reality. There is then nothing for it but to show my own fragile I and stake it on the game.

When I was making *Writer*[14] in Detroit, I visited an author. He kept exploring the boundaries between us, the interviewer and the interviewee, pushing further and further, while I was recording everything with my clearly visible microphone. The tension kept on building and turned real and dangerous. At a given moment I pointed a gun, that I held, along with my mike, in my sweaty palms, at his chest. 'Right in the chest. C'mon. Chest! Not arm. I write.

I need my arm. Do you want to do the interview? Do you want to do the fucking interview? Pull the trigger.'

The sweat was real, my fiery cheeks were real and my quavering voice was real. I was I in that moment, but at the same time not. I was also, my specific I, my producing I, and my narrative voice, which later manages the dramatic arc during editing and the poetry of the story. In the course of our conversation the writer quoted *The Love Song of J. Alfred Prufrock*, T.S. Eliot's well-known poem, and in a hair-raising way I was dragged into a reality that started very much to look like that in the poem. Eventually the poem became the filter that I imposed on reality, in order to make the chaos and unease into a story.

Telling your own story, is one of the most empowering things a person can do. Every time we do it, we have control over what has happened to us.

'I think every time we have an opportunity to tell our own story, we wield power over what has happened to us in our lives', says Kaitlin. 'We get to say what happened from our point of view. And a tiny bit of weight gets lifted from your shoulders.'

Recently Jonathan Goldstein's *Heavyweight* podcasts give his stories and his voice to persons both known and unknown, in order to figure out together with them what keeps them awake at night. In passing he lets the listener see his thoughts, and how things affect him. Alan Hall creates a framework for voices that he regards as being more important than himself, so that they can be heard. For Rikke Houd this framework is the poetic filter that she imposes on the world to create meaning. In my own case, the framework is the narrative mechanism that creates the necessary distance for analyzing the situation. The framework makes room for the experience and the emotions of the narrator who has experienced it, and gives the listener the space to witness the events and the developing thought processes.

When, however, I as the narrator am also the I who has experienced everything, I have the authority to stand in the place where the narrator is the most vulnerable, and I can appeal directly to the empathic powers of the listener. The real danger though lies in sentiment, or the reduction of real events and people to easy narrative lines. With this in mind, I am able, by availing myself of documentary resources, the rules of narrative, and the artistic mechanisms that are available when making audio stories, to use the fragile I as a powerful narrative instrument. I can, via my documentary work, try to understand the world better and use my subjective insight to communicate as honestly as possible with the listener. As I am myself present in the recorded scenes and use the I narrator in my own voice, I must also relate truly to reality. I can only partly hide behind the net of story structures or a produced, poetic version of myself. In its pristine form recorded reality is sometimes incomprehensible, uneasy, inscrutable. But with my honest involvement and subjective point of view I can in all honesty try to make a story out of what appears to be chaotic and meaningless. Without concealing my personal imperfections and vulnerability, I can, by telling the story, gain responsibility over the reality. Even if I am half-naked, my microphone is the weapon with which I dare to stand in the middle of the road.

A podcast version of this text in Dutch can be found on www.forum-online.be.

Notes

1 Peter Handke, *A Sorrow Beyond Dreams*, trans. Ralph Mannheim (London: Pushkin Press, 1974).
2 Ibid., p. 3.
3 Ibid.
4 'Falling Tree Productions', www.fallingtree.co.uk (accessed 25 March 2018).
5 Tim Crook, *The Radio Drama* (London: Routledge, 1999), p. 64.
6 All quotes from respectively Alan Hall, Rikke Houd, Jonathan Goldstein, and Kaitlin Prest are my own translations and were drawn from interview and conversations I have had with them.
7 Rikke Houd, http://rikkehoud.dk (accessed 25 March 2018).
8 Bill Nichols, 'Documentary Reenactment and the Fantasmatic Subject', *Critical Inquiry* 35, no. 1 (Fall 2008), pp. 72–89, www.jstor.org/stable/10.1086/595629. (accessed 25 March 2018).
9 Handke, *A Sorrow Beyond Dreams*, p. 42.
10 Katharina Smets, *Senza Parole*, radio documentary, Holland Doc Radio on NPO Radio 1, 16 February 2014.
11 Wilma de Rek, 'Roem, een belangrijk thema in het werk van Connie Palmen', *de Volkskrant*, 18 March 2017, www.volkskrant.nl/boeken/roem-een-belangrijk-thema-in-het-werk-van-connie-palmen~a4475605/ (accessed 25 March 2018).
12 Jessica Abel, 'The Heat of Their Breath: Character and Voice', in *Out on the Wire: The Storytelling Secrets of the New Masters of Radio* (New York: Broadway Books, 2015), p. 101.
13 'The Heart', *season: no* (2017). Kaitlin explores her sexual boundaries from youth to adulthood, http://www.theheartradio.org/no-episodes/ (accessed 25 March 2018).
14 Katharina Smets, *Detroit Detour*, radio documentary, VPRO Woord on NPO Radio 1, 20 February 2015.

Fiction as a Visual Strategy in the Photobook

How Contemporary Photographers Challenge the Documentary Genre through the Printed Page

Stefan Vanthuyne

> All literary forms are artificial, and they are constantly changing, to match the new tone and mood of the culture.
> V.S. Naipaul, *The New York Review of Books*, 23 April 1987[1]

> Everything is put there with one goal, which is to tell the story in the best way possible, no matter what.
> Laia Abril, at the symposium 'The Individual, The Political and The Photobook', 1 February 2018

At the 'Photobook Phenomenon' in CCCB in Barcelona in 2017, an exhibition on the role of the photobook in contemporary visual culture and as a way to reinterpret the history of photography, there was a space dedicated to contemporary photobook practices. Mexican photographer Alejandro Cartagena had written a text on the wall, next to a presentation of spreads of his book *Santa Barbara Return Jobs back to US* (2016), the first in a trilogy on the current state of affairs in America. In this text, which is also printed in the exhibition's catalogue, he clearly and eloquently addresses the issues and the challenges documentary photographers face today, and why they increasingly turn to making books. According to Cartagena, the photobook opens up a space to explore the possibilities of narrative in documentary photography. Instead of being constrained to the structured assignment, where the images one creates need to visualize the subject of that project, Cartagena believes that those constraints can be modified and played with through the photobook, pushing the idea of documentation to another level of experimentation, doubt, and questioning of form and content. 'In essence', Cartagena concluded,

> we are constructing new meanings and suggesting a point of view that, yes, might be flawed or biased, but it is also the starting point for a more thoughtful and broader manifestation of something that might deserve a little more of our time, money and attention.[2]

The exhibition also featured the most recent book by Barcelona-based Laia Abril. *Lobismuller* (2017) is a historical story, told from a female perspective, of an enigmatic Spanish serial killer. A project that according to the artist, 'moves slightly away from documentary photography, towards reconstruction, documentary fiction or art'.[3] The book is based on Abril's factual research, which she then conceptualizes, connects, and visualizes. Abril adds what she calls layers of visual and production research, visual inputs from sources, which often have nothing to do with photography or with the story itself. Three years earlier she had published the critically acclaimed *The Epilogue*, where she carefully reconstructed the story of the Robinson family, and the aftermath of losing their 26-year-old daughter to bulimia. Abril had already been working on what she refers to as the world epidemic of eating disorders since 2010.

Both Cartagena and Abril participated in a round-table discussion during the symposium 'The Individual, The Political and The Photobook' on 1st February 2018, on the role of the contemporary photobook in the documentary genre of photography today. Through thorough attention to design, image selection, and sequence, photobooks have become a perfect medium for complex and layered visual stories. And in what has become a noticeable trend, more and more photographers experiment with the book in terms of both form and content to push the ideas and boundaries of the documentary genre. Besides Abril and Cartagena the panel consisted of Belgian photographer and doctoral researcher in the arts Max Pinckers, who had just self-published his fourth book *Margins of Excess*, where again he questions notions of truth and fiction in documentary photography, this time in what we now call a post-truth era.

Fictions of an Imagined Truth

The round-table discussion opened with the cover image of Max Pinckers' latest book. That image–a black boy in a white T-shirt holding a white girl in a black shirt, the girl having tears in her eyes, in a dramatically lit scene–is part of a series of images that are woven through the book and that come back every so often. Pinckers made the images in collaboration with young actors in Hollywood and in New York. This idea stems from his research at the KASK School of Arts Ghent, where he is investigating stereotypes, the conventions, and the recurring images that we tend to see in photojournalism or news photography. Research that also resulted in the making of the Trophy Camera v0.9, 'the first prototype of an A.I.-powered camera that only makes award-winning pictures',[4] based on all previous winning World Press Photos of the Year.

One of the things Pinckers is interested in, he said during this discussion, is how after an event–mostly horrific events, like a bombing or a tragedy–newspapers and media need to start producing images to tell the story. Often, we see very similar images being published; people putting flowers near a memorial or people hugging each other, pictures that are very emotionally charged and are often close-ups. Pinckers wanted to investigate if he could recreate this type of imagery, but without anything actually having happened. Working with actors, 'who can cry on demand', Pinckers aimed for an emotional effect on the viewer, in a similar way as the press might do when selecting images for their news stories.

In the book, Pinckers connects six different American stories, all situated somewhere in the realm between truth and fiction, into one narrative. Most of the time the subject matter dominates the narrative, Pinckers pointed out. When making a documentary work, people will talk about the subject, rather than the visual strategy or the visual approach. Pinckers' oeuvre until now has always been about finding a new balance in which the subject matter and the visual approach are in constant dialogue. Working with six different subjects instead of one, meant that none of them could dominate what the work was about.

The six protagonists are real people, not actors. However, one of them, Herman Rosenblat, had died in 2015, a year before Pinckers started photographing. Rosenblat became known for the so-called Holocaust love story, a story about how he met his wife. In 1993 Rosenblat wrote a memoir, entitled *Angel at the Fence*. In one scene a young and hungry Rosenblat, who was held captive at the Schlieben subcamp of the Buchenwald concentration camp, recalls how a young girl threw him an apple from the other side of the barbed wire fence. Twelve years later he recognized the girl in a woman called Roma Radzicki, with whom he was on a blind date in Coney Island. Soon after, the two got married.

The memoir was set to be published in 2009, but the release got cancelled when it became clear that much of what Rosenblat had written was fabricated, something he admitted to after appearing on *Oprah* in 2007. According to the *New York Times*, Rosenblat had lied because he

> wanted to bring happiness to people, to remind them not to hate but to love and tolerate all people. ... My motivation was to make good in this world. In my dreams, Roma will always throw me an apple, but I now know it is only a dream.[5]

In his imagination, he believed it, Rosenblat said. 'Even now, I believe it, that she was there and she threw the apple to me.'[6]

Pinckers is concerned with what happens and what the consequences are when these personal stories, these fictional truths that were created in someone's imagination for no harmful reasons, start to take on an unexpected and uncontrollable life of their own, once they are uncovered by the media. In the book, Pinckers replaced the apple with an orange. While on the road, doubt struck about whether in fact it was an apple or an orange. Pinckers and his wife Victoria, who accompanies and assists him on his projects, eventually choose an orange, because of the bright contrast against the blue sky; the title of the resulting image being The Apple That Wasn't. The fact that the apple was already a figment of Rosenblat's imagination gave Pinckers the necessary space to make this kind of aesthetic decision as a photographer, he told in an email. For a portrait of Rosenblat he used a stand-in, an old man that could be any old man, his head turned away from the camera, with an apple in his hand. Here Pinckers is using fiction to recreate a truth that was imagined in the first place. It's a delicate balancing act, he admits, but that is exactly what makes it so interesting.

In a somewhat ludicrous way, all of this is reminiscent of the Wildlife Photographer of the Year 2017 controversy, where a winning photograph entitled *Night Raider* was disqualified because the animal in the picture turned out to be dead. The Natural History Museum in London, which runs the competition, consulted five independent scientists to conclude that the anteater in the photograph was in fact stuffed.

In a wonderful opinion piece in *The Guardian*, David Mitchell writes that the viewer has been deceived into inferring that the anteater is alive. But then again, he argues, it doesn't really misrepresent the reality of nature, as 'anteaters do attack termite mounds–he [the photographer] just failed to capture it actually happening'.[7] Fiction is the lie through which we tell the truth, Mitchell quotes Albert Camus. 'Well, if *Night Raider* is a lie, and it tells the truth about anteaters, is it fiction? Yes.'[8]

If an anecdote turns out to be fictional, Mitchell writes, people lose interest in it. The stories in *Margins of Excess* however are more, or became more than simple anecdotes, some of them causing people to feel betrayed, sometimes even outraged. Because what was only a personal fiction at first, suddenly became a public lie; and in the case of the unlikely Rosenblat love story, a lie people really wanted to believe.

A Narrative License

Within the history of photography, the use of fiction through staging is not new. In his essay 'Documentary Fictions', Joan Fontcuberta discusses the famous picture with a view of the Boulevard du Temple, a daguerreotype from 1838 made by the inventor of the process, Louis Daguerre. Shot from a window in Daguerre's apartment, looking out on the Boulevard, the image is considered to be the first photograph of a person. According to Fontcuberta there were two identical shots, taken from the same point on the same day, but at slightly different times. The first photograph shows a seemingly empty Boulevard devoid of all human presence, not because there were no people roaming the streets of this vibrant centre of Parisian theatre, but the long exposure time needed–fifteen minutes to sometimes more than an hour–simply erased all moving figures and objects. To obtain a sharp image, anyone on the street would have to hold still during the entire time of the exposure.

The second picture however, the one that would eventually gain its place in the history of photography, comes with a small surprise, showing the presence of a bootblack and his client on the pavement in the lower left corner. The scene not only looks incredibly perfect; it also feels rather convenient. So convenient that Fontcuberta suspects Daguerre, who had theatrical experience, of having hired two actors, perhaps his assistants, 'to simulate a situation that is static but not without a certain naturalness'.[9] Yet, here too we would love to believe that the bootblack just happened to be there at the right moment, holding is still for long enough. According to Fontcuberta, not in the least because it makes for a better story.

The strictly documentary use of the camera fails in its attempt to capture living reality, and it is only by cheating that we can achieve a certain truth, only with a conscious simulation that we come close to an epistemologically satisfying representation.

> That this is a form of fraud ... shifts the question to one of value judgments and an ethical code that determines which behaviours are licit. We can regard it as narrative licence, as well-intentioned mischief, or as a rhetorical resource of

> information whose ultimate basis lies on the political horizon of its consequences.[10]

American photojournalist W. Eugene Smith stirred a small controversy when it became known that many of the most famous shots from his photo essay *Spanish Village*, published in *LIFE* magazine in 1951, had in fact been staged or re-shot by him. In an interview during an American Society of Media Photographers meeting in 1956, when asked about the possible staging of one picture of a woman throwing water in the streets, Smith answered that he would not have hesitated to ask her to throw the water, adding that he doesn't object to staging if and only if he feels that it is an intensification of something that is absolutely authentic to the place.

When colleague and interviewer Philippe Halsman then asks him why he breaks this basic rule of candid photography, Smith delivers his famous quote: 'I didn't write the rules–why should I follow them?'[11] Since he puts a great deal of time and research to knowing what he is about, Smith said he asks and arranges if he feels it is legitimate. 'The honesty lies in my, the photographer's, ability to understand.'[12] Fontcuberta not only follows this line of reasoning, as his thoughts on Daguerre's picture suggests, he also stresses that knowing this does not in any way devalues Smith's humanistic and artistic merit. 'I've always thought that the photographer does artistic work and that art consists of working with fictional premises.'[13]

This is indeed the established context in which contemporary artists such as Pinckers, Cartagena, and Abril work today, one would assume. And in a way one could say it is what separates the artist from the photojournalist, though boundaries concerning this distinction are–and will probably always remain–blurry, and because of that, occasionally contested. Pinckers was accepted as a nominee to the prestigious Magnum agency in 2015, but he didn't pass the vote to become an associate member two years later. In Pinckers' view, the majority of photographers still have a traditional view on documentary photography, where staging is still taboo. During the symposium Pinckers rephrased this opinion as follows:

> As an artist, we are always trying to look for a way to be completely free, to be able to do exactly what we want to do without having to explain ourselves, without having to contextualize it. We just want to make the images we have

> in our mind. But of course, that's very difficult. It's all about finding a balance between how much you have to bring a context into it–or a narrative, or some kind of way that someone who can't read your mind can still reflect on it or find something in it for themselves.

Editing and Sequencing, Patterns and Structure

When Alejandro Cartagena started to work as a photographer, conceptual expectations were high. The work always had to start with a well-defined project 'and a text that explains what you're trying to do', dixit Cartagena. For six or seven years, he tried to fulfil the expectations of the text with images. In a next phase, he turned things around. Though he still created a context to work in, he didn't start from a fixed conceptual framework before he photographed. Instead, he wanted to photograph first, and then afterwards, through the process of editing, create meaning. For his Santa Barbara-trilogy–including *Santa Barbara Return Jobs back to US* (2016) and *Santa Barbara Shame On Us* (2017), part three still to come–Cartagena worked as a resident in Santa Barbara in 2015, making photographs and collecting a lot of images; everything that had to do with the city. He only had one month to take pictures. Being used to taking three to four years for a project, he felt anxious and scared. Embracing this anxiety, he started what he calls an anti-documentary project. After this short residency he used the internet as a camera for several more months. He would type 'Santa Barbara' into a search engine and he would just browse, download, and gather images. He also went down to the Library of Congress and looked for anything on Santa Barbara.

> And then suddenly Santa Barbara became nothing. Because there's Santa Barbara everywhere: there's a Santa Barbara in California, there's one in Mexico and one in Chile–there are many Santa Barbaras. That brought to me a question: who's putting the meaning to places and to things? (Cartagena during panel discussion)

Cartagena realized it was a project that was not bringing answers and was not telling you something, it was asking questions. Only afterwards, working with the editors of the book, he understood what had happened. He took the pictures in 2015 during the presidential election campaigns in the US. These for him were ideal circumstances; nobody knew what was going to happen. This complete uncertainty is reflected in the pictures and thus the book also reflects the uncertain cultural state. So here again the question of meaning pops up: the images were taken a year before, but when thoughtfully edited, they talk about the state of a place, of a situation today.

Part two of the trilogy dealt with the fact that Trump actually won the elections, making Cartagena wonder what the current feeling was of this American culture when somebody that more than half of the US didn't want as a president wins. So, they edited these images–which had nothing to do with the elections or the current conditions–in such a way that it felt like they were talking about people's feelings right here, right now in the US. The trilogy will end at the end of Trump's term, where no one yet knows what will happen. But the pictures have already been made and have been gathered. So again, the authorship, Cartagena says, will come in trying to talk about what is going to happen in three more years, using images made five years ago.

Editing and sequencing images lies at the very core of photobook making. It is often a long and hard process of looking for relationships and patterns, relying not only on chronological or visual connections between photographs, but also making use of symbols and metaphors. One of the clearest explanations about how sequencing–and what he calls image binding–works in photobooks, and how this relates to fiction, was written by Tate Shaw, director of the Visual Studies Workshop in Rochester, New York:

> I'm using the word *binding* in the conceptual sense, how images mentally link to one another or to a text. Photo sequence combines images in a specific order to create a context for meaning to be inferred between the images... . Binding compels the reader to give the two images a single overriding identity and recognize them as a whole. A narrative leap is required to see the two pictures as one entity. To form a closure, we think through why they go together, though this thought process may not be entirely conscious. ... Metaphor expresses a complex idea by making a comparison, one thing to another, to more clearly represent the unrepresentable. Binding the subject matter in these two distinct images becomes a way the photographer can make what is interior exterior. Image binding is a fiction the author creates by having one photograph

> following another in sequence. The strength of fiction is that it is unreal, and yet it exists in the world to reveal something about it. Part of reading fiction is forgetting that you're doing it. You have to unconsciously see through the ink on the page to experience a barely budding awareness outside of what is actually there.[14]

According to American photographer Doug DuBois, author of *All the Days and Nights* (2009) and *My Last Day at Seventeen* (2015), when a photobook begins to happen, the story in a sense has already been written. When the process of converting the work to a book starts, it's all about structure. 'And structure is very much about pattern and of course pattern generates meaning.'[15] Filmmaker Wolf Koenig took this idea one step further when speaking about the demanding editing process of documentary films–which shares certain similarities with the process of editing and sequencing a photobook–by not only also stating that structure is what a film is really about, but also aligning it with truth:

> I've come to the conclusion in my dotage that 'structure' is what all the arts are really about–music, dance, the graphic arts, the theatre, the literary arts, architecture, poetry, etc. They show us by inference something that we otherwise can't see. This 'something' is invisible to us, like a fir tree in the dark. But come Christmas time, people hang lights all over the boughs. At first one only sees the lights, but if you step back a bit and squint, you see the shape of the tree–even though the tree itself is still invisible. The lights define it, so we're able to see it by inference. In this laboured analogy, the lights represent the 'arts' and the tree the 'structure'. And the structure is what permeates the universe from the sub-atomic particle to the whole cosmos–in effect, we are all little lights hung on the invisible tree. And the arts are about the only way we have of talking about this thing: structure or truth.[16]

Notice also how both Shaw and Koenig respectively speak of 'a barely budding awareness outside of what is actually there' and showing us 'by inference something that we otherwise can't see'. This idea very much relates to what Cartagena referred to. Except that in his case, the events on which the stories are based are yet to unfold, though the images with which they will be written, have already been made, making these stories fictions about a future present, edited in such a manner that they will speak of a present state when published.

In a fascinating way, Cartagena's trilogy becomes a contemporary conceptual example of what John Berger wrote in 1982, in an essay on photographic stories, on the process of sequencing—and by extension on the idea of a personal authorship.

> Photographs so placed are restored to a living context: not of course to the original temporal context from which they were taken—that is impossible—but to a context of experience. And there, *their ambiguity at last becomes true*. It allows what they show to be appropriated by reflection. The world they reveal, frozen, becomes tractable. The information they contain becomes permeated by feeling. Appearances become the language of a lived life.[17]

Visual Codes and Strategies

Next to being staged, edited, or sequenced, images and how they are read are also influenced by visual codes. Max Pinckers uses these visual codes in his work to counteract what is expected from documentary photography. From very early on in his work, Pinckers uses these codes in an aesthetic or formal sense, for instance by not only staging a scene, but also lighting it in a theatrically way that is reminiscent of advertising:

> In advertising we presume that we are being sold something, because of the form the image has and because of the lighting, because of the codes advertising uses. Whereas in photojournalism we assume that we look at something that really happens, and this too involves visual codes. I think aesthetics play a very important role in that. If we see images on the internet from protests, amateurish video footage that is more pixelated, then we assume that it is more real, because it feels more transparent. (Pickers during panel discussion)

Thinking about how aesthetics play a role in making us believe certain things about what we are seeing, Pinckers attempts to bring these different forms together, to create new interpretation through the conflict that arises from this, always in function of what he wants the viewer to believe, or to make the viewer reflect on what he is told to believe.

Spanish artist Laia Abril has a background in journalism, and her work is primarily research-based. Even though she never really worked much as a journalist, the ground of what she does is still based on facts. Documentary photography however had put her in a box, she felt, and even though she tried to get rid of this objectivity issue, it was always there. Wanting to shed light on hidden issues that are disturbing and uncomfortable, documentary photography didn't allow her to tell the stories that she wanted to tell, because most of the time these issues are invisible. This was especially the case with *On Abortion*, published in 2017 and the first chapter of a new long-term project called *The History of Misogyny*. In the colophon in the back of the book she writes:

> This project is a visual analysis and interpretation by the artist of the repercussions of lack of access to abortion in the world. Some of the images in this book are reconstructions or visual metaphors based on information discovered through extensive research.[18]

This was the first time Abril had reconstructed images, while talking about a very real subject, thus reacting against everything she'd been taught. Talking about reality, fiction, and documentary photography, she said at the round-table, she doesn't really have a strong opinion on what we should do. She does know however that she needs a reality behind the story that she's telling, but that reality doesn't necessarily have to be reflected in the images. Mostly because it doesn't exist anymore, because the events in the story have happened in the past.

After her studies, Abril had first moved to New York, and then to Italy where she ended up in Fabrica, a communication research centre based in Treviso, and an integral part of the Benetton Group. Abril worked for five years as a photo editor, photographer, and researcher for their magazine *Colors*. Here she was surrounded by designers and creative people and not in touch anymore with the world of documentary photography. Founded by advertising photographer Oliviero Toscani, design is the most important aspect of the magazine, before photography and before text.

At this point she decided to also work on photobooks. One of the first books Abril designed and edited, together with Ramon Pez, with whom she worked for her own books as well, was *The Afronauts* (2012), an immensely successful self-published book by Cristina De Middel, an old friend of hers. 'The way we started doing photobooks was very similar to the way we did the magazine', Abril recalled. 'Design, production, budget, narrative, storytelling... Everything is put there with one goal, which is to tell the story in the best way possible, no matter what.'

During a workshop she gave to photography students at the Royal Academy of Fine Arts Antwerp, Abril spoke about how *On Abortion* doesn't really contain any graphical images, even though she had seen disturbing photographs herself, and had access to these images, but specifically decided not to show them. Like Pinckers, she found herself looking for visual strategies, in which she tried to avoid stereotypical images of victimization. Nonetheless there were a couple of images that were very important to her. One is about a woman who had died in the fifties, a rather graphic image of her lying dead. She had just had an abortion, and she passed away. Abril decided not to use the picture in an exhibition. But she considered the book as a different experience, a more intimate and slower one. Reading a book, she felt, is less physical than being in a public space with other people, looking at these images–that's hard. You can close the book, think about it and come back later. Abril turned to design as a way to include the image in a non-confrontational way. She decided to place the image behind another image–in order to see it one needs to lift the upper image. It is also printed in a very transparent way so one can barely see it. The tone of the book is very subtle; it is the way Abril thinks the story should be told.

Another way of guiding the reader, then, of course, is the use of text. Especially when the subject of the story is hard to photograph, because it is invisible or it concerns a past event, text becomes very important. One of the most interesting things about the photobook format is that it provides room to really contextualize the images and the sequence, using other materials than photographs, dixit Max Pinckers, who deliberately uses text as a tool to steer the reader in a certain direction or interpretation. 'If you want to tell a reader exactly where they have to go, you need text', Cartagena added. 'Images can't do that.' Without any additional context photobooks remain incredibly open to interpretation. The first time Laia Abril used words it was not in a written text. Instead she used a voice in an interview in a multimedia installation. She also considers the use of words, either written or spoken, as a strategy, a way to subtly move somebody from the first page of the book to the last one.

Whatever story is being told or whatever theme or subject is being communicated, or whatever the intention with which it is being communicated, many of the strategies or methods photographers use are intended to hold the reader's attention, to guide them in a certain direction according to a well-thought-out path, whether or not with the help of an editor, a designer, or even a publisher.

The Photobook Maker as Author as Producer

The more strategies are being used, one could argue, the further one goes astray from the facts and the closer one comes to fiction. John Berger, in that same essay on photographic stories wrote: 'In reports ambiguities are unacceptable; in stories they are inevitable.'[19] Today however, for photographers such as Pinckers, Abril, and Cartagena, ambiguities have become instrumental; albeit remaining, in the spirit of W. Eugene Smith, something to be dealt with, with great responsibility, care, and consideration.

As Pinckers pointed out during the round-table, the documentary space is a very interesting one, precisely because there is always that presumption that we are referring to something that really happened, something that is real, something that is important for our reality. 'Documentary as a genre doesn't have a very distinct form that we can identify, so there is still a lot of room for how you can go about using that space.' The importance of an inventive and artistic approach within that space today, is also emphasized by David Campany. He writes that with no agreed conventions to fall back on, documentary has now entered a state of permanent and urgent experimentation: 'One cannot assume the form one's work should take: one discovers it idiosyncratically, in the midst of things.'[20]

The books themselves become important instruments through which their makers reflect on media and visual culture, on a level that surpasses the stories they contain. They address issues of documentary photography and the status quo, and the need for critique and self-reflection. In a glorious review of Laia Abril's *On Abortion*, critic Jörg Colberg recognizes this critical but constructive potential of the photobook:

> With a world of photojournalism mired in what looks like a morass of problems (gender, diversity, Western-centric views, various photography problems), from which it is unable to extricate itself, *another world is possible.* And that is what Abril presents with *On Abortion*: she establishes the new gold standard of the research-based photographic book.[21]

This attention to form and strategies in art within a present political climate is the point of focus in a speech prepared, but never delivered by Walter Benjamin for the Institute for the Study of Fascism, a Communist front organization in Paris, in 1934. The title of this speech was 'The Author as Producer'. In the text Benjamin examines the relation between the production of literary works and the politics of the time in which they are produced. 'This question directly concerns the function the work has within the literary relations of production of its time. It is concerned, in other words, directly with the literary *technique* of works.'[22] Benjamin directs our attention to Russian writer Sergei Tretiakov, who made the distinction between the operating writer and the informing writer. While the informing writer merely reports, the operating writer wants to intervene actively. Benjamin sums up an array of activities that Tretiakov, whom he considered an operating writer, performed in 1928:

> ... calling mass meetings; collecting funds to pay for tractors; persuading independent peasants to enter the *kolkhoz* [collective farm]; inspecting the reading rooms; creating wall newspapers and editing the kolkhoz newspaper; reporting for Moscow newspapers; introducing radio and mobile movie houses; and so on.[23]

Benjamin then had planned to defeat his audience to the demur that these tasks had more to do with journalism and propaganda than with literature, with which they seem to have little to do, by stating that he cited the example of Tretiakov deliberately:

> ... in order to point out to you how comprehensive the horizon is within which we have to rethink our conceptions of literary forms or genres, in view of the technical factors affecting our present situation, if we are to identify the forms

> of expression that channel the literary energies of the present. There were not always novels in the past, and there will not always have to be; there have not always been tragedies or great epics. Not always were the forms of commentary, translation, indeed even so-called plagiarism playthings in the margins of literature; they had a place not only in the philosophical but also in the literary writings of Arabia and China. Rhetoric has not always been a minor form: in Antiquity, it put its stamp on large provinces of literature. All this is to accustom you to the thought that we are in the midst of a mighty recasting of literary forms, a melting down in which many of the opposites in which we have been used to think may lose their force.[24]

Looking at the documentary genre within photography today, one can argue that it is in a similar state of recasting as literary forms were, during an intense political period in 1934. In a similar vein, photobook makers such as Max Pinckers (working with facts and fiction in a post-truth era), Laia Abril (working on misogyny and women's rights) and Alejandro Cartagena (looking at the US under Trump) can be considered authors as producers, resorting to the book as their medium of choice and to creative strategies–the technique of the work, in Benjamin's words, which refers to both the aesthetic choices and the means of production–that indeed perfectly fit these times. And here too, the works of these photographers are not protest or propaganda books, nor are they a form of journalism in the strict sense of the word.

According to Benjamin the writers that matter are the ones that are the best technicians in their fields. 'An author who teaches writers nothing teaches no one', he claims. 'What matters, therefore, is the exemplary character of production, which is able, first, to induce other producers to produce, and, second, to put an improved apparatus at their disposal.'[25] Does the writer have 'proposals for the *Umfunktionierung* of the novel, the drama, the poem?',[26] Benjamin asks near the end of his speech.

Max Pinckers, Laia Abril and Alejandro Cartagena–and other contemporary photographers with them–deal with documentary photography as genre, in terms of its function, and the photobook as form. These authors, as producers, are playing with the photobook, pushing the idea of documentation to another level of experimentation, doubt, and questioning of form and content, as Cartagena wrote on the wall at the 'Photobook Phenomenon' exhibition. This is indeed something worth talking about, because photographers, designers and publishers are making these books as we speak.

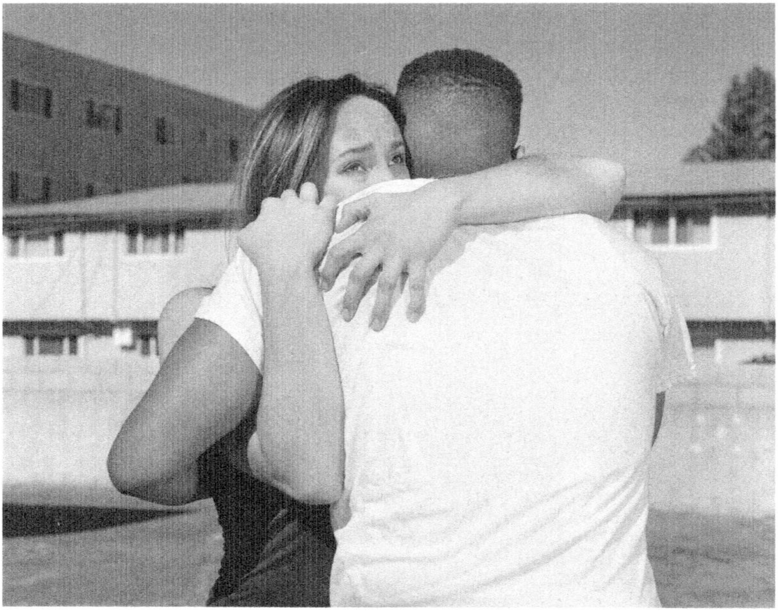

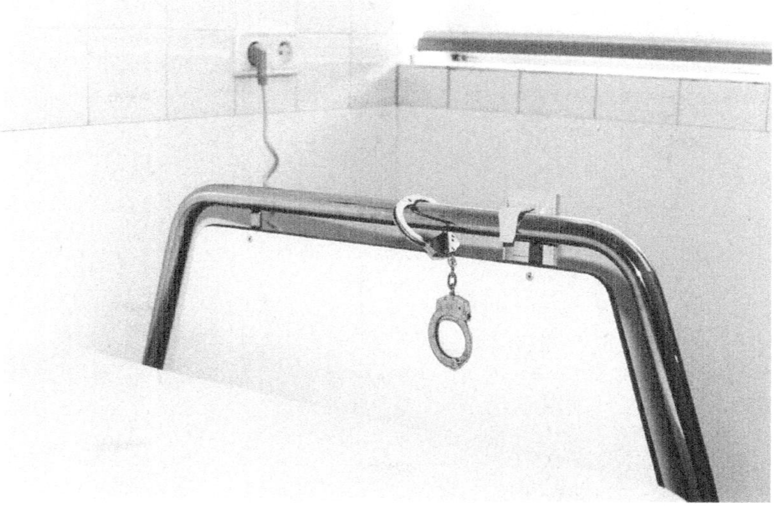

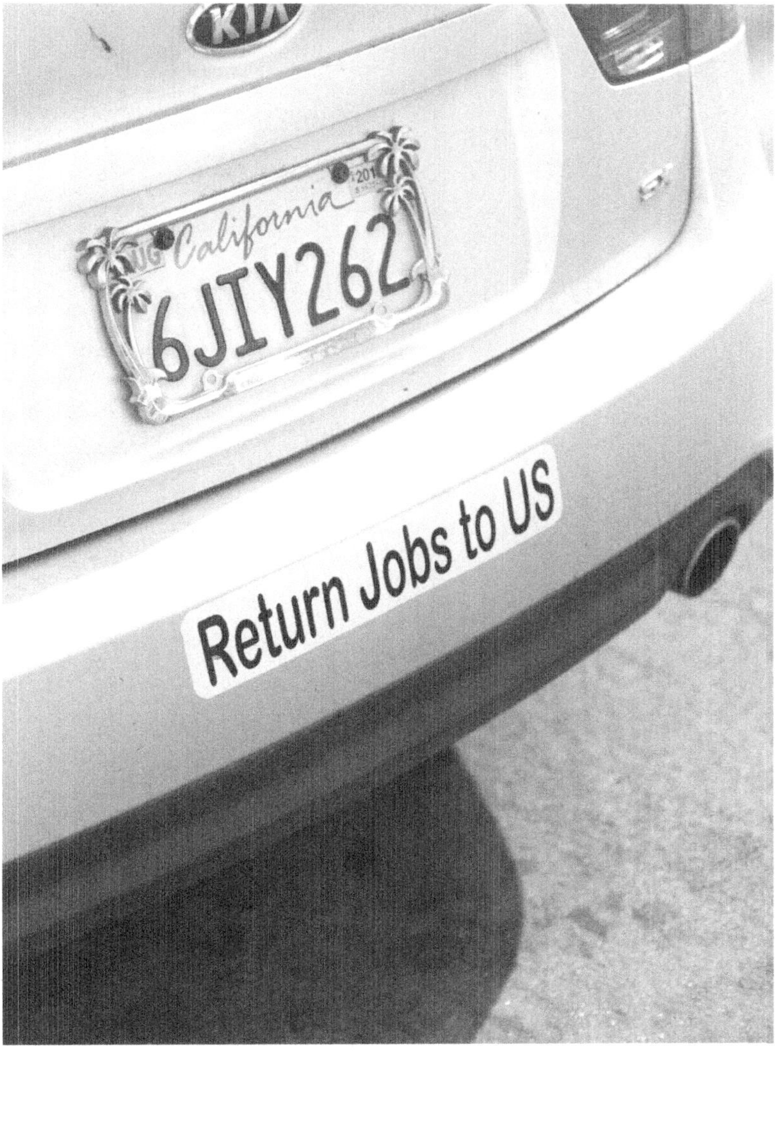
KIA
California
6JIY262
Return Jobs to US

Images

- From *Margins of Excess* © 2018 Max Pinckers
- From *On Abortion* © 2016 Laia Abril
- From *Santa Barbara Return Jobs Back To US* © Alejandro Cartagena

Notes

1 V.S. Naipaul, 'On Being a Writer', *The New York Review of Books*, 23 April 1987, www.nybooks.com/articles/1987/04/23/on-being-a-writer/ (accessed 28 August 2018).
2 Alejandro Caragena, 'Santa Barbara Return Jobs back to US, 2015–16', *Photobook Phenomenon: Contemporary Practices*, ed. Irene de Mendoza and Moritz Neumüller (Barcelona: CCCB/Fundació Foto Colectania/RM Editores, 2017).
3 Laia Abril, 'Lobismuller, 2016', *Photobook Phenomenon: Contemporary Practices*, ed. Irene de Mendoza and Moritz Neumüller (Barcelona: CCCB, Fundació Foto Colectania, RM Editores, 2017).
4 'Trophy Camera v0.9', Max Pinckers, www.maxpinckers.be.
5 Sam Roberts, 'Herman Rosenblat, 85, Dies: Made Up Holocaust Love Story', *The New York Times*, 22 February 2015, www.nytimes.com/2015/02/22/business/media/herman-rosenblat-85-dies-made-up-holocaust-love-story.html (accessed 28 August 2018).
6 Ibid.
7 David Mitchell, '"If you must fake a photo, it had better be good"', *The Guardian*, 6 May 2018, www.theguardian.com/commentisfree/2018/may/06/if-must-fake-photo-better-be-good-stuffed-anteater-wildlife-competition (accessed 1 September 2018).
8 Ibid.
9 Joan Fontcuberta, *Pandora's Camera* (London: MACK, 2014).
10 Ibid., pp. 108–109.
11 'W. Eugene Smith: "I Didn't Write the Rules, Why Should I Follow Them?"', *The New York Times*, 3 March 2013, https://lens.blogs.nytimes.com/2013/01/03/w-eugene-smith-i-didnt-write-the-rules-why-should-i-follow-them/ (accessed 28 August 2018).
12 Ibid.
13 Christina Zelich, 'Joan Fontcuberta: Interview with Christina Zelich//2005', *Documentary*, ed. Julian Stallabrass (London: Whitechapel Gallery/MIT Press, 2013), pp. 180–183.
14 Tate Shaw, 'Strategic Linkage: Binding and Sequence in Photobooks', *The Photobook Review*, ed. Markus Schaden (New York: Aperture, 2012), p. 4.
15 Tom Griggs, 'Interview: Doug DuBois, Part II', *Fototazo*, 18 February 2013,

www.fototazo.com/2013/02/interview-doug-dubois-part-ii.html (accessed 29 August 2018).

16 Wolf Koenig, 'On Editing and Structure', in *Vision Anew: The Lens and Screen Arts*, eds. Adam Bell and Charles H. Traub (Berkeley: University of California Press, 2015), pp. 104-105.

17 John Berger, 'Stories', *Understanding a Photograph*, ed. Geoff Dyer (London: Penguin Books, 2013), pp. 99-104.

18 Laia Abril, *On Abortion* (Stockport: Dewi Lewis, 2018).

19 Berger, 'Stories', p. 99.

20 David Campany, 'Best Books 2015: David Campany', *Photo-eye*, 8 December 2015, http://blog.photoeye.com/2015/12/best-books-2015-david-campany.html (accessed 3 September 2018).

21 Jörg Colberg, 'Photobook Reviews W08/2018', *Conscientious Photography Magazine*, 2018, https://cphmag.com/reviews-w0818/ (accessed 3 September 2018).

22 Walter Benjamin, 'The Author as Producer', *Selected Writings Volume 2, Part 2, 1931-1934*, eds. Michael W. Jennings, Howard Eiland, and Gary Smith (Cambridge, MA: Harvard University Press, 1999), pp. 768-782.

23 Ibid., p. 770.

24 Ibid., p. 771.

25 Ibid., p. 777.

26 Ibid., p. 780. *Umfunktionierung* refers to the term refunctioning, an aesthetic strategy Bertolt Brecht implemented in his theatre, because he wanted it to intervene in the shaping of society. Brecht wasn't just concerned about form and content, but about content, form (or technique) and function.

Linus' Blanket
Visualizing the Economy of Fear

Charlotte Lybeer

Since 2003, Belgian photographer Charlotte Lybeer has been photographing the experience of life today in a highly artificial world. Her early works focus on the staged and controlled environments of gated communities and theme parks. She portrays people who define their identity through codes and masquerades, demonstrating membership of one group while distancing themselves from mainstream society.

Lybeer photographs subcultures that are related to virtual three-dimensional worlds, where players construct a second identity online. These trans-human identities also adopt their avatars outside the virtual world. Lybeer's photographic projects thus visualize how people respond to a changing world: a world that expands geographically, but also increasingly in the realm of the imaginary. In these series she captures the isolation and stillness of her subjects, their escapist desire to become the character of a dream, shaped by film, virtual reality, and games.

In her recent series *Linus' Blanket* (2017–2018) Lybeer focuses on the influence of the culture of fear on the world of entertainment. Nowadays, we are flooded by national and international media with concepts such as safety, prevention, and the importance of limits. But what does this mean? Safety is a concept that encompasses a number of measurable parameters. At the same time, it has strong emotional connotations. Human beings apparently are strongly inclined to minimize the objective factors of insecurity as best they can through societal choices, policy actions, regulations, employment conditions, and personal decisions. On the other hand, fleeing is also a strategy in which a place (a concrete or a mental space) is sought that is apparently safe and that is also protected against the intrusion of risk factors of any kind. This kind of escapism is a central theme in Lybeer's recent photographic work.

In this series, Lybeer portrays members of groups who wish to eliminate danger through so-called 'preventive actions' and try to protect themselves against both known and unknown threats. In addition, she zooms in on places where the ecology of fear slowly creeps into the everyday. This results in a series of photos from the best secured chips shop, to combat simulation sports, to a course in 'falling safely'... Lybeer shows the façades of these systems where one can periodically escape to and 'exercise' in self-protection in a controlled setting, or is it rather fleeing? After all, the images simultaneously illustrate the current need for protective barriers, the desire for a safe cocoon into which people can withdraw. The artificial anxiety that is evoked in recreational entertainment and the imminent danger of the world outside with the associated defensive reflex, become remarkably similar.

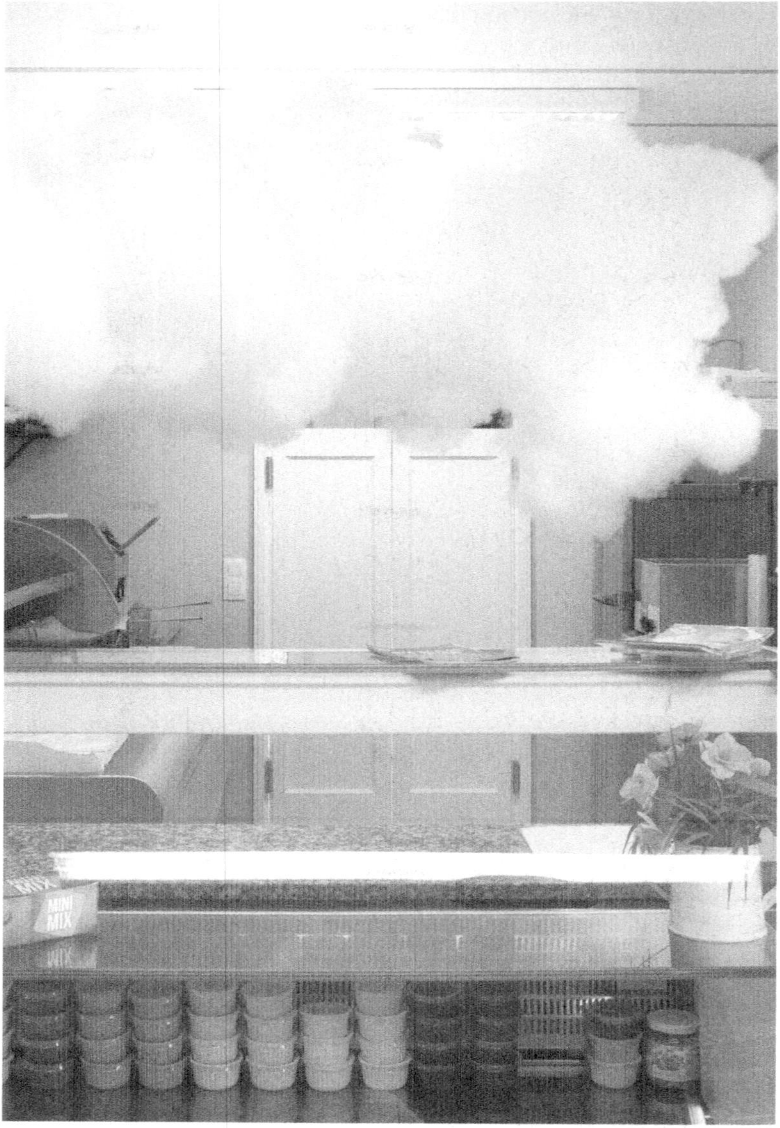
MINI
MIX

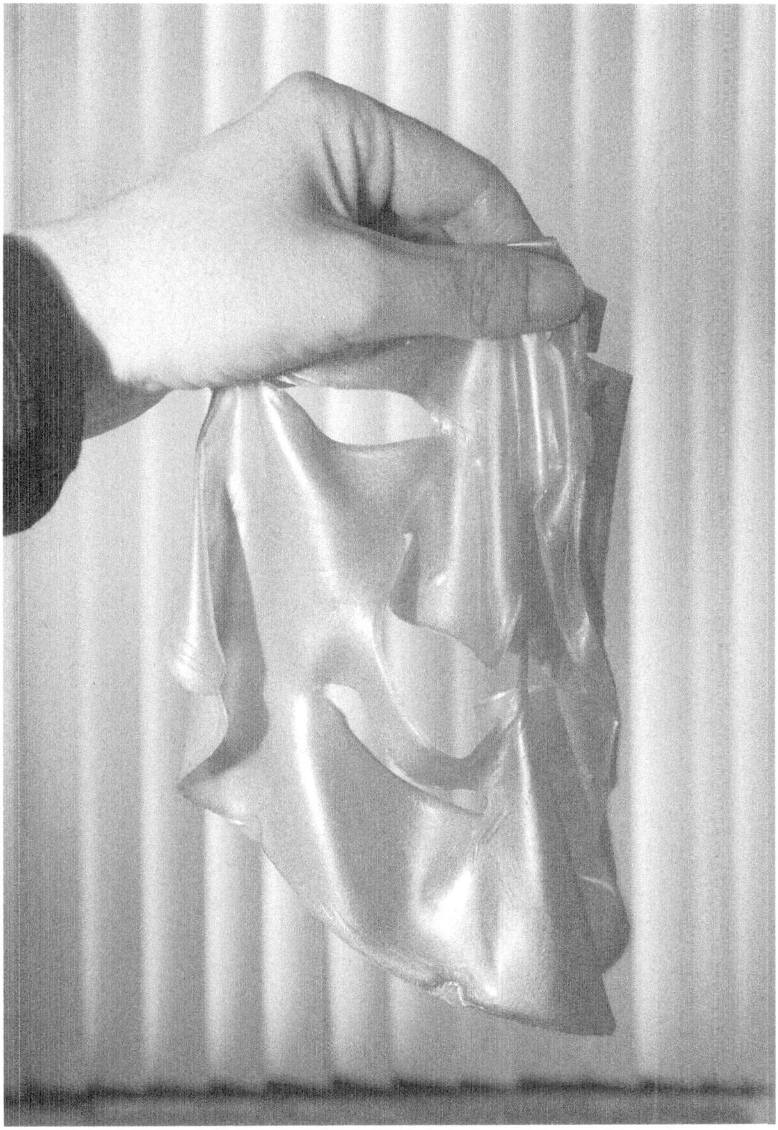

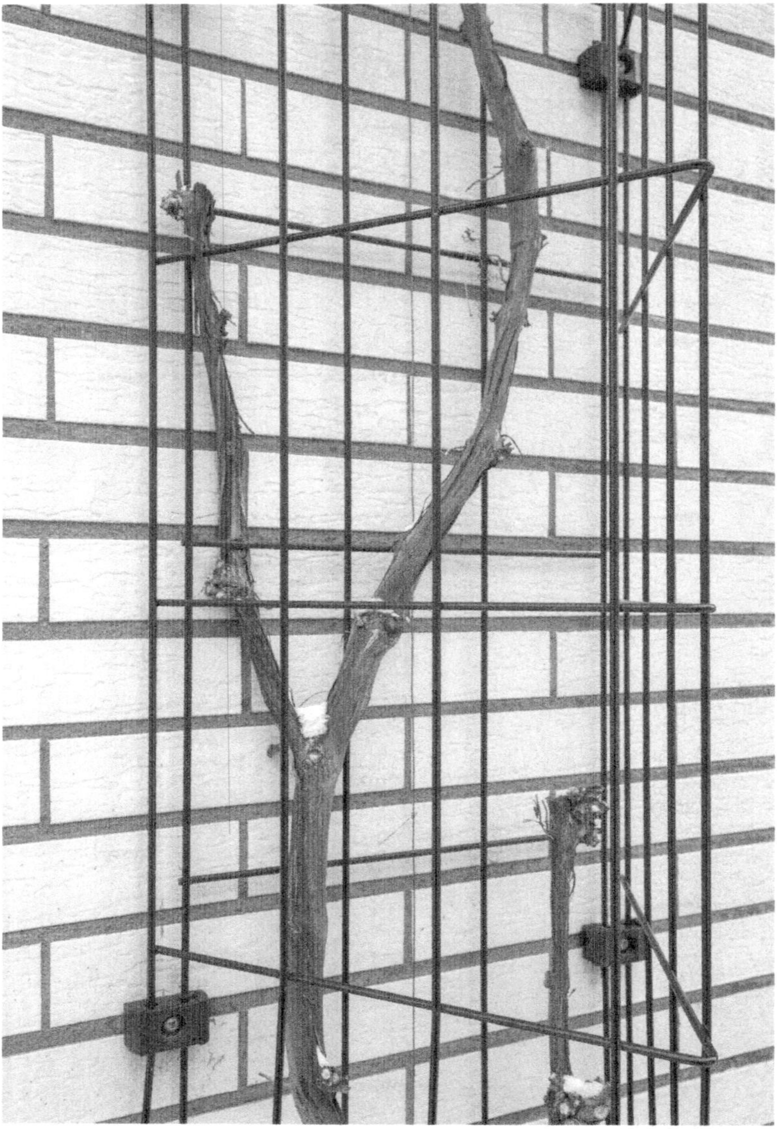

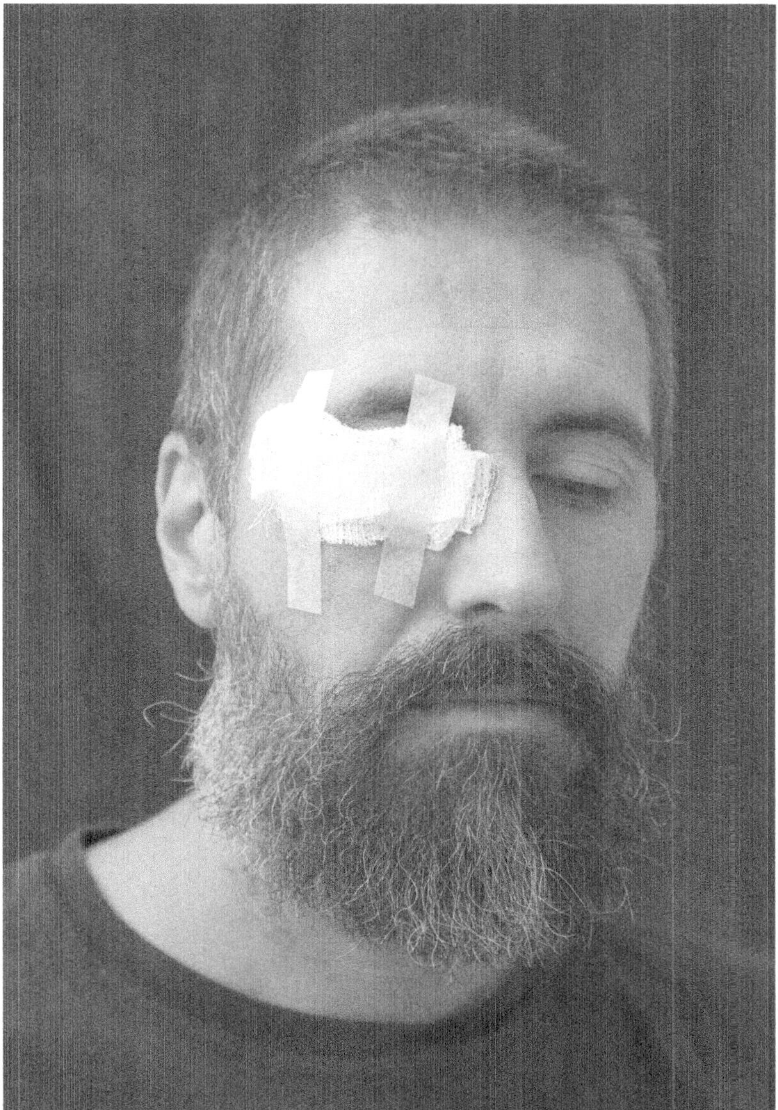

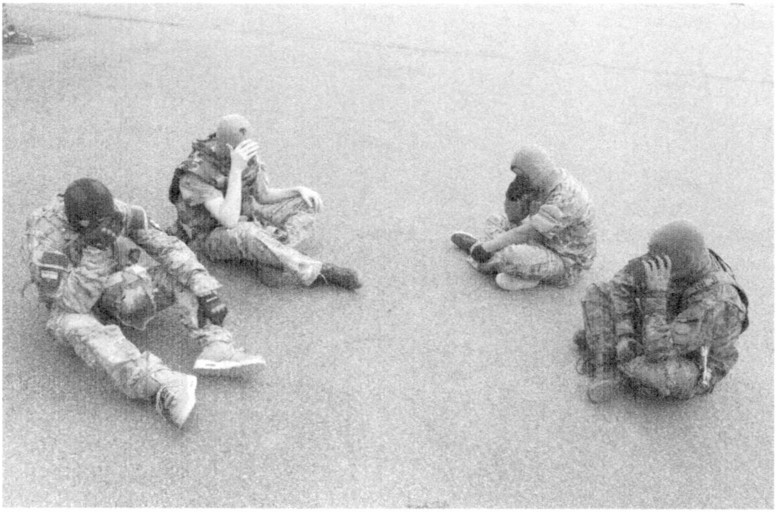

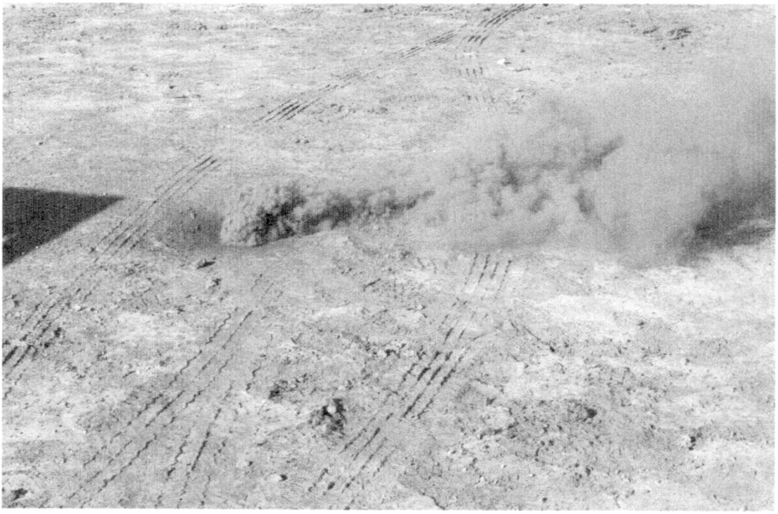

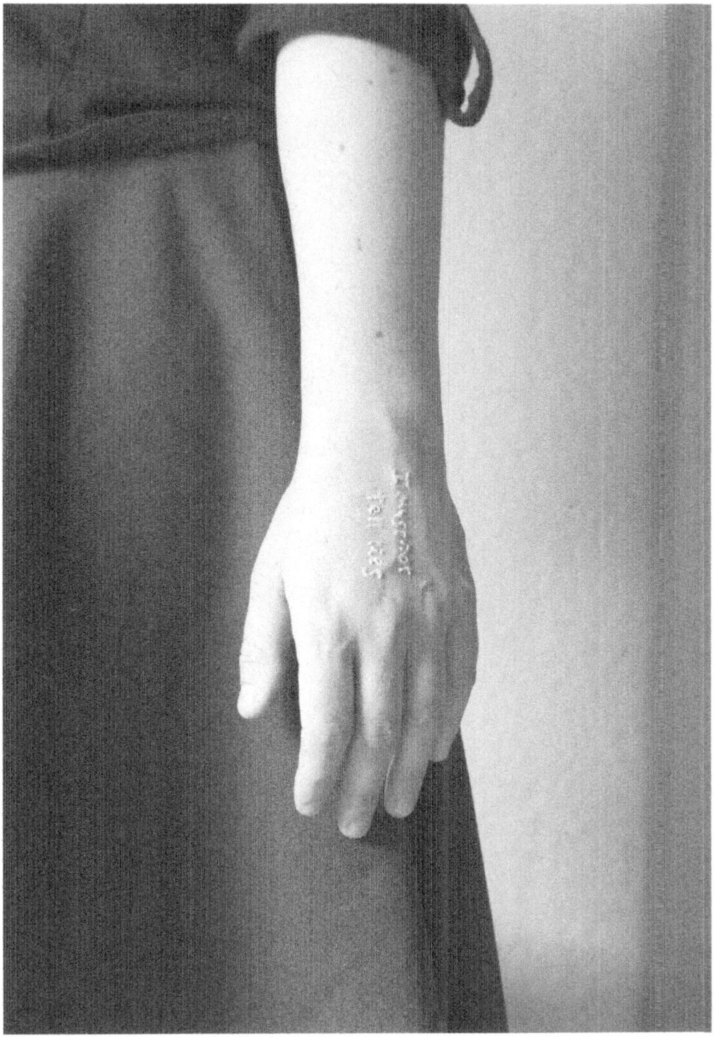

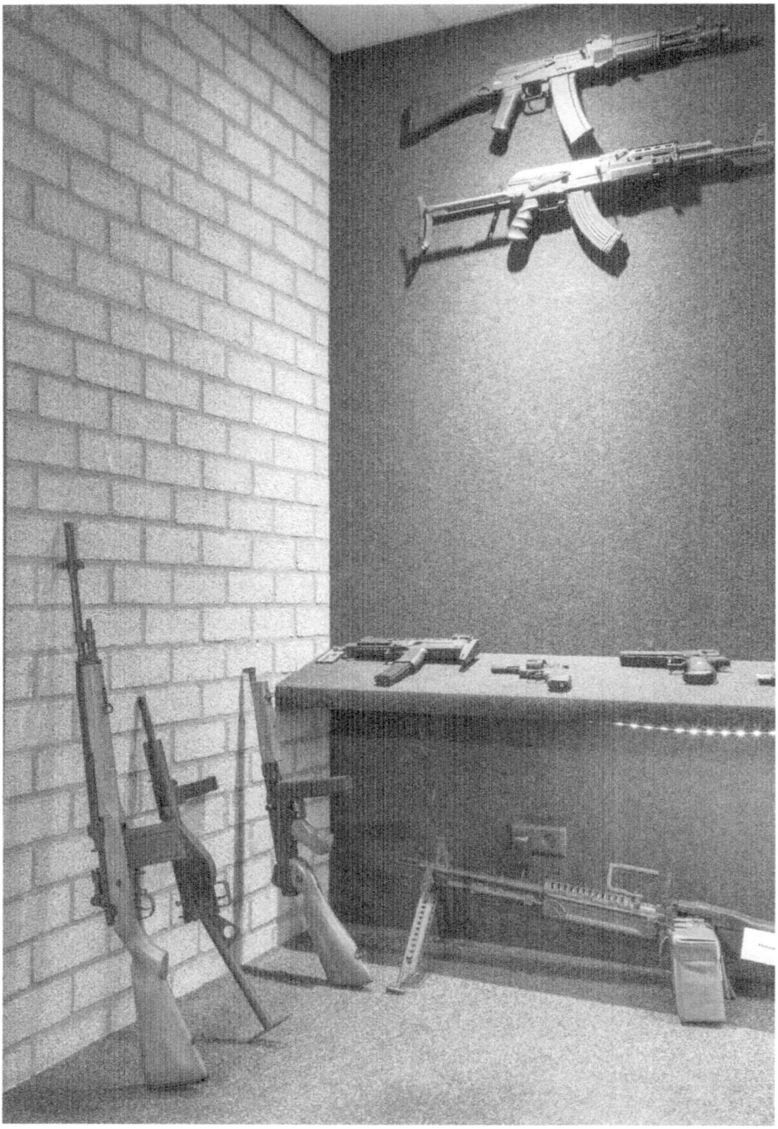

Images

- *Smoke Curtain + Anti-Pollution Mask*, from series *Linus' Blanket* (2017-2018) © Charlotte Lybeer
- *Plant Cage + Barry* (2017), from series *Linus' Blanket* (2017-2018) © Charlotte Lybeer
- *Airsoft Players*, from series *Linus' Blanket* (2017-2018) © Charlotte Lybeer
- *Bomb Blast*, from series *Linus' Blanket* (2017-2018) © Charlotte Lybeer
- *Lies + Gun Room*, from series *Linus' Blanket* (2017-2018) © Charlotte Lybeer

The Case of the Ridiculous Curator

Andrea Gorki in Conversation with Ludovik Vermeersch

I've met a young French poet here. I'm amazed and excited about the calm, objective, modest, and clear way he writes and thinks about art. He's very interested in my work and he will write about my drawings.[1] Ernst Ludwig Kirchner in a letter to Ernst Gosebruch on 21 January 1920[2]

How We Met

Ludovik Vermeersch: During the summer of 2017, Andrea Gorki approached me with a long and obsequious email containing a request to meet with me. She announced a plan to make a lecture performance about my work as a curator. 'I would be thrilled if you...' etc. A couple more e-mails followed, each less composed than the previous ones. 'Not sure if my e-mails are getting through', she wrote. What better signal than my silence could I have sent her to make it clear that I wasn't interested? She asked whether an interview over the phone would work if meeting in person was too difficult.

In her first letter, Gorki had introduced herself as a visual artist. I looked her up on the internet, but found no clues as to her artistic activities. A few weeks later I received another email, which came with a premature sketch of her lecture. This document shed some light on her intentions and showed that she was hoping to 'deconstruct' my work. Nothing in her writing particularly excited me, her explanation was sometimes difficult to follow. Her choice to target my person, apparent already from her working title, was based on the wrong premise. 'Which part of you is staged', she wanted to know, 'and which part is authentic?' She seemed more interested in the construction of my persona than the artistic position that my work represented.

I'm not opposed to criticism, but I don't feel obliged to assist every would-be critic of mine with extensive interviews. I thought it wiser to let Miss Gorki figure out my work as if I didn't exist. If my voice nonetheless features in the following conversation, I hope Gorki manages to reach the 'point where only language acts, "performs", and not "me"', as a French philosopher once wrote.[3]

Andrea Gorki: I first met Ludovik Vermeersch on 2 April 2017, after he had just given a lecture performance on abstract art at me Collectors Room Berlin.[4] Vermeersch had long grey hair, a ferocious beard, and impressive eyebrows. His charismatic stage presence contrasted with a surprising air of uncertainty in person. When I approached him to introduce myself, he was slightly evasive. He had earned himself a cigarette, he said, and he didn't invite me along as he hurried outside.

Vermeersch lectured with an intensity of expression unlike the cautious, academic attitude that curators nowadays display. But he managed to make the demanding content of his ninety-minute talk digestible–somewhat of a tour de force. Vermeersch's opening question was: Why is abstract painting still so popular in the twenty-first century? His answer: because of the audience's desire to indulge in some form of veneration. Let me try to summarize his argument.

Finding the roots of abstraction in ornament, Vermeersch identified 'dysfunctional referentiality' as the main ingredient of abstract art. By generating mystery, confusion, and ambiguity, abstract images could draw the viewer into a state of not-knowing. Leaning on the mystical theology of Pseudo-Dionysius, Vermeersch argued that the bewilderment experienced by the viewers would enhance their desire to be initiated into a higher level of knowing, to witness some form of revelation, thus creating the conditions for a cult of the image. To achieve this effect nowadays, however, the abstract painter could not rely purely on shapes and colours. To successfully draw the viewers into a 'puzzled involvement', the artist had to turn narrative into an accomplice of her subversion.

To demonstrate his theory, Vermeersch gave a detailed account of his collaboration with six young abstract artists in Berlin. Over the course of two years, he had coached them 'to move away from their obsession with formal abstraction and to concentrate on achieving a contextual abstraction'. The way Vermeersch prioritized his own theoretical agenda at the expense of the artists' personal investigations was questionable. And it was equally puzzling why the artists hadn't shown any signs of resistance.

Towards the end of the lecture, the suggestion was raised that one of the six artists, Jens Presser, was in fact the architect of the project. Presser, it was insinuated, had invented the five other artists, as well as their work. By implication, Ludovik Vermeersch himself was just a character in Presser's scheme and the lecture was just a parody. But you couldn't be sure. Although Presser was present that evening, he didn't provide conclusive evidence in support of this thesis. After the performance, the artist participated in a conversation with Vermeersch and art historian Rahel Schrohe. The discussion was entirely scripted. Presser read his part from a paper, occasionally stumbling over a sentence, which made it hard to figure out what was actually going on—probably an intended effect of the 'contextual abstraction' Vermeersch sought to establish.

Several months passed and my confusion still lingered. I kept referring to this intriguing event in conversations. I bugged my artist friends with the tedious doubts that painters typically have about painting—doubts reawakened by Vermeersch's lecture. Feeling compelled to respond to this peculiar curator, I started working on a lecture performance of my own.

When I wrote Vermeersch, he immediately agreed to meet and to discuss the topics in his work that I found problematic. I gave my lecture the working title 'The Ridiculous Curator' in the spirit of what Vermeersch had termed 'pseudo-iconoclasm'. I think he enjoyed that subtle provocation. He gave constructive comments when I showed him a draft of my lecture performance, which was eventually presented in Antwerp and Berlin in the spring of 2018.[5] Many people were intrigued. They asked, who on earth is this Ludovik Vermeersch?[6] One reaction was surprising. 'The parts where you describe your interaction with Vermeersch sound a bit contrived, you mention too many details', a young man told me. I've since cut down on the details. I hope it's more convincing that way. Still, even if I invented my meetings with Vermeersch, they may nonetheless furnish our understanding of his persona and project. Imagining a person's reasoning, getting inside their head, putting oneself in their shoes can sometimes be more revealing than asking them to explain themselves.

The Charismatic Narcissist[7]

AG: Thank you for taking the time to talk with me. As you know, I saw your lecture performance *Personally, I'm Most Interested in the Shapes and Colours* in Berlin and it left me somewhat devastated. I felt that your method of 'transfigurative recontextualization' humiliated the artists you worked with. As an abstract painter, I was drawn to your talk because it was announced as a discussion of 'abstract art's continued potential as a disruptive practice'. But I don't think anyone who saw the lecture would have thought: 'Gee, I'm going to buy myself some brushes and start painting shapes and colours.' Quite the opposite. If I may be frank, there was something destructive in the way you approached the painters' creative process, something vicious that went way beyond simple irony.

LV: I see what you mean. I don't think it was vicious, though. I admit that it's a bit provocative to continuously remind the audience of painting's futility when you're introducing a group of painters. However, my point was that focusing only on the formal qualities of a painting is inconsequential if you want to create a disruptive experience for the viewer. You have to work with the narratives surrounding the works! Some form of destruction was necessary to make this point. Iconoclasm is part and parcel of all truly innovative projects. Even if some of my artists took a bit of time to digest my provocations, I'm sure they got something out of it. It's no use making art if you don't manage to develop an indestructible confidence in what you do.

AG: Have you spoken with the artists since the project's conclusion?

LV: Jens Presser is the only one I've regularly spoken with.

AG: Wouldn't it be interesting to follow up on their work?

LV: None of the others seemed too excited to stay in touch.

AG: Did your book and lecture benefit their careers in any way?

LV: I don't think so. Jens has accompanied me on a few presentations. He seemed to enjoy the project a lot.

AG: What if your attempts at innovation lead to a point where the destruction is beyond repair?

LV: You're overestimating my powers as a curator. The artists can take my suggestions or leave them. If someone doesn't agree, he'll move on. Also, there's nothing worse than an artist who doesn't believe in his own work. Whichever strategy you choose, you have to be dead serious about it.

AG: The philosopher Boris Groys defines the curator as an iconoclast, as an 'agent of art's profanation'.[8] Comparing the curator's powers to those of the artist, he concludes: 'The independent curator is a radically secularized artist. But he is an artist who has lost the artist's aura, who no longer has magical transformative powers at his disposal, who cannot endow objects with artistic status.'[9] Do Groys' ideas resonate with your experience as a curator? Do you consider yourself an artist?

LV: In a way, Groys perpetuates the structuralist idea that not only the writer but also the reader should be seen as an author. I share this belief, and it rightfully invalidates the conventional distinction between the artist as the one who creates, and the curator as the one who merely selects. Ever since Marcel Duchamp created his *Fountain* by pseudonymously signing a urinal, the act of selecting the right object is enough to turn you into an artist. But Groys wrongly assumes that this expanded definition of authorship is reflected 'de facto' in an expanded range of options from which the public chooses when they identify 'the author' of a work of art. He thinks it's an accomplished fact that nowadays we detect a collective authorship, where in the past, we would only have seen a traditional 'sovereign' author at work.[10] That is wishful thinking. Sure, the notion of individual authorship is a myth. But that's no reason why we'd stop seeing it everywhere and believing in it. The illusion is way too appealing.

AG: I'm not sure I follow you. If I make a painting, I'm the author. Why would that be an illusion? It's not like I have a group of assistants working for me.

LV: I don't agree. We all have assistants. If you're a painter, it starts with the anonymous people who make your canvas, the company that produces your oil paints, the manufacturer of the camera you use to make the pictures you laboriously copy, with brushes that come from China. There's the nude model who may agree to pose for you, the teacher who tells you what can be improved, your fellow painters whose ideas you steal, the intern who writes the press release for the gallery that puts your name in its window, and so on. There's an endless chain of people who are never named but who are your co-authors. And I'm not even mentioning the accomplices you need in order to assert your authorship over the things you believe you created when you're on your way to becoming famous.

That all this is not already obvious to you shows how difficult it is to dismantle the illusion of the single author. So here's the twist: I'd be nothing but a bore if I kept trying to debunk that illusion. That's why I'm promoting another strategy, that is: to embrace the myth, along with the narcissism that underlies it. So, to answer your initial question: yes, I do consider myself a kind of artist, but I don't buy Groys' analysis. Of course, there are curators who fit his definition just fine. Think of the exhibitions that Anselm Franke stages at Haus der Kulturen der Welt here in Berlin. But I'm different, I keep striving for the transfiguration of the commonplace, to use Arthur Danto's words. I see myself as an enlightened mediator of art's magical powers. And in the project we're talking about, I even go beyond that role. I'm offering an aesthetic experience that the artists are unable to create by themselves.

AG: The question is whether the experience you create doesn't come at the expense of the artists' individual works.

LV: That is only worrisome if you truly believed in the fiction of individual authorship!

AG: But you've just said you decided to advocate this fiction.

LV: No, I said I advocate the idea that we should embrace this fiction, while being conscious of the fact that it is a fiction.

AG: Isn't that the same thing?

LV: Not at all. The latter option is the enlightened one. It's like the difference, say, between promoting God as a real entity and promoting Him as material for a good story, knowing that He doesn't exist. You see, here's an ambiguity that I haven't fully come to terms with myself: I don't mind destroying the nicely framed image of the single author to let the viewers know they're being fooled. But deep down, I'm too eager to stick my own head through the emptied frame and say, look here, I'm the authority!

AG: That's very candid. You said that narcissism underlies the fiction of the single author. Does that also apply to how you've just analyzed yourself? Can I compare your persona to Narcissus? Maybe to a Narcissus who is aware of his delusion, who knows he is looking at his own reflection, but is unable to break the spell?

LV: I've called myself a 'pseudo-iconoclast' on several occasions, exactly because I'm aware of the dialectics of iconophilia and iconoclasm.[11] The need to destroy images is mostly rooted in the strong conviction that they have a harmful effect. That they seduce you, for instance, to believe in the wrong God. So, the iconoclast acknowledges the power of the image at least as much as the iconophile. And when, eventually, the iconoclast starts putting the results of his destructive actions on display, he's just creating the icons of a new regime. That's also what Groys' 'profane' curators do. As far as narcissism goes... I'm just trying to avoid your question (*laughs*). No, I don't really have a problem admitting my narcissistic streak. But when I mentioned narcissism before, I meant it more metaphorically. I don't want to argue that all artists are narcissists. Although I'd have to admit that they often display the symptoms.

AG: Any examples?

LV: I don't know. Just look around. Or take the latest book by that journalist who travelled around the world asking famous artists: 'What is an artist?'[12] It's full of quotes about omnipotence, magical powers, the urge for unconditional love... In psychoanalysis, the artist is seen as a pathological narcissist by definition. Think of Otto Rank. Almost a hundred years ago, he thought it was a necessary condition for every artist of some importance to systematically overestimate his own powers and to withdraw into the delusional belief that his art was the highest of all.[13] Of course, this is absurd, and this is not the point I want to make. It is possible, however, to apply this diagnosis to the social construction that is 'the artist'. You could argue that a structural narcissism is embedded in society's understanding of what it entails to be an artist. The way society celebrates the ultimate singularity of a select group of artists reflects the desires of a collective narcissistic libido. Unrestrained by rational considerations, inebriated with narcissistic lust, the collective gives in to the urge to adorn some of its members with a highly exceptional status. The bogus image of the successful artist kindles in certain young people the budding of an artistic calling. They lose their mind and choose to devote their life to art. A heroic gesture, you'd almost say.[14] I'm exaggerating slightly (*laughs*). But you see my point. The desire to become an artist is grounded in the illusion of sovereign authorship.

AG: So even if you could, you wouldn't necessarily want to demythologize the special status of artistic creativity. You don't want to blow out the flame that keeps it going. You want to keep intact the idea of an undefinable quality that gives the 'outstanding' artist the power to transfigure objects into art.

LV: Very well put, Miss Gorki. Naturally, we all know it's the institution that anoints the artist, that grants him this supposed power. A power that turns out to be very fragile, by the way. Yet the illusion that the artist himself, or herself, is ultimately responsible for these transfigurations is an incredible source of uplifting energy for the self. And thus, why not embrace this particular understanding of authorship? In the late seventies, Pierre Bourdieu called this the 'charismatic ideology'.[15] Today, even with the advent of artistic research, this ideology still dominates the art world.[16] How could you possibly counter that?

> I tell [Jeff Koons] that I am fascinated by artists' personas. The author of an artwork is part of its meaning, is he not... I've asked you about your persona twice, I say, and you have evaded the question twice.
> Sarah Thornton[17]

The Extended Self

AG: In the closing chapter of your lecture performance, you showed a video that featured Jens Presser, the most 'playful' of your six artists. However, he was a different person from the Presser who had appeared in an earlier video. This Presser sounded much more authoritative. He claimed that the other artists had been his alter egos. It was as if a veil had been lifted and the truth was exposed. But you were quick to deny his statement. It had just been another layer in your narrative, staged to sow confusion. At the end, you put your own authority into question by suggesting that you might very well be a fictional character and that you were, after all, 'performing a script'. That suggestion was then played out in the conversation that followed: the text was read from a sheet of paper and you didn't say much anymore. The audience left the event wondering whether they had missed a crucial piece of information. Was the whole set-up of the lecture fake? What about the artworks? Were they merely props? Two decisive elements for the viewers' aesthetic judgement were thrown overboard: the attribution of authorship and the possibility of affirming the authenticity of what they had seen.

LV: All true. But what do you want me to say to that?

AG: There's a paradox in your project. Your lecture tried to criticize and hinder the audience's tendency to identify the author of an artwork. Yet, you've now made it clear that in your own position as an author or curator, you're unwilling to give up that same self-centred perspective. It wouldn't be so hard to find more sincere ways of putting your critique of authorship into practice. I'm thinking of collaborative art projects or anonymous artist collectives like the Guerrilla Girls. You're not taking that path, because you seem obsessed with what you're trying to criticize. You introduce the concept of the alter ego in order to play a game of hide and seek that may be enjoyable for whoever is pulling the strings, but that doesn't resolve the desire that underlies the 'charismatic ideology'.

LV: I never contradict a good paradox. This one draws us deeper into our discussion of narcissism. I'd have to return to Otto Rank. You may think I'm his biggest fan, but that's not the case. Have you read Dostoevsky's story *The Double*?

AG: I think I have.

LV: It's one of many stories from the nineteenth century that feature the phenomenon of the Doppelgänger. Rank wrote a book about this literary figure. You may laugh, but what did he find the double's emergence symptomatic of? Narcissistic fixation! The narratives always follow a similar pattern: a protagonist, characterized by a lack of *Liebesfähigkeit*, creates a second self that is much more charming, knowledgeable, and successful than his first self. In the beginning, the double appears as his benevolent accomplice, but soon he develops into his most intimate rival. The stories then usually end on a destructive note. The same goes for Dostoevsky's novel, where the main character, Yakov Petrovich Golyadkin, is eventually sent to an asylum. Dostoevsky serves you the story in a particularly powerful way, because as a reader, you're never sure if Golyadkin's confusion is the result of his imagination or if the double is actually real. His state of mind is transferred to us: we're uncertain of what exactly is going on. This leads us into the mental state of 'active discovery', as Monroe Beardsley termed it.

AG: So the mechanism of doubling doesn't actually offer a useful escape route, but it creates an interesting aesthetic experience?

LV: Precisely! As a solution to the narcissist's problem, the double is hilariously unhelpful: you're so fixated on yourself that the only way out of your obsession seems the creation of a second self. The second self may be less obsessed with himself, and possibly more concerned with the world. Unfortunately, the latter self only exists in your imagination! So, creating a double doesn't amount to a clever attempt at escape from the self. You might turn paranoid, just as Golyadkin did. However, as an artistic strategy–and here we move far away from the pathological–the double can become a very interesting device, especially when you want to challenge the public's tendency to confuse the author with his work and draw misguided conclusions. The funny thing here is, when you look at examples of artistic alter egos, you can sometimes see how the pathological dynamic of the double plays out in them. I've actually written an article on this subject.[18]

AG: I saw that, but it's in Dutch.

LV: A recent example is Joe Scanlan. His alter ego stirred up considerable debate. In the early 2000s, Scanlan created the persona of an African-American woman named Donelle Woolford. You'd almost think the white Ivy League professor Scanlan had designed her to cause himself trouble. But by the time her presence at the 2014 Whitney Biennial finally led his critics to accuse him of insensitivity to gender and race inequalities, this seemed to take him by surprise.[19]

Or take the poet Ern Malley. A very interesting case. In 1944, the Australian poets James McAuley and Harold Stewart concocted a scheme to ridicule their colleagues on the avant-garde spectrum of the scene, who didn't show much interest in their conventional poetry. One afternoon, the duo invented a poet who had died young and had left the world seventeen poems, one of which was unfinished. His name was Ern Malley. In a frenzy of vexed inspiration, the anti-modernist gentlemen created Malley's body of work in just a few hours, using the avant-garde methods of collage and *écriture automatique* that they despised.[20] They made the deceased poet's fictional sister send the poems, along with a sketch of the young man's tragic biography, to the avant-garde poetry journal *Angry Penguins*. The editor of the journal, the poet Max Harris, immediately recognized in Malley an experimental genius, and devoted the next edition of the magazine to his discovery.

Shortly after the poems' publication, the hoax was revealed. Remarkably, Harris didn't budge. He remained convinced and defended the quality of Malley's work. Several modernist critics, among them Herbert Read, spoke up in defence of the poems. To every true avant-gardist, this story was proof of how effective surrealist and dadaist methods were, regardless of the author's actual intentions. The alter ego, sent on a mission to expose the innovators' useless criteria, had defected to the other side. Malley's posthumous oeuvre of seventeen poems eventually became more influential and more famous than the rest of McAuley's and Stewart's work. Half a century later, Harold Stewart felt the need to comment that 'perhaps neither McAuley nor I ever existed except in the imagination of Ern Malley'.[21]

AG: That's a great story.

LV: Isn't it? But my favourite one is that of the French writer Romain Gary. With Gary, a deep motivation becomes apparent. Deeper than the ocean's deepest waters. He played the game of the alter ego with extremely serious devotion. His case may sound pathological, but he managed to lift his subterfuge into the realm of art. You see, this man was famous. He had won the Prix Goncourt in 1956 with *Les racines du ciel* (*The Roots of Heaven*). He was a celebrity, he married the film star Jean Seberg in the sixties. But in the early seventies, his star began to wane. He felt trapped in the straitjacket of stereotypes the media had put him in. 'On m'avait fait une gueule', he would later write.[22]

So what did he do? He decided to publish a novel under the pseudonym Émile Ajar, to see whether he could free himself from his image. The book, *Gros-Câlin*, appeared in 1974 and was an immediate success. Gary felt that journalists would request interviews with Ajar, so he employed his nephew Paul Pavlowitch to play the role of his alter ego, initially just as a voice on the phone. Their collaboration would go on for seven years and was only put to an end by

Gary's suicide. The dynamic between the author and the performer of his alter ego was exemplary of Rank's schema: it went from innocent complicity to mutual suspicion and rivalry.

Initially, Pavlowitch, who was a passionate reader, was eager to participate in what Gary called his 'roman total'.[23] But as their collaboration developed, and Gary finished the manuscript for Ajar's second novel, *La vie devant soi* (*The Life Before Us*), Pavlowitch started to put more and more of his own personality into the role. When the author decided that Ajar needed a public face, this produced a fundamental disagreement: Gary wanted Pavlowitch to use make-up and to disguise himself to avoid identification. But Pavlowitch, wanting to be more than just a pawn in his uncle's game, sent out a photograph in which he was clearly recognizable.[24]

It didn't take long before a journalist tracked Pavlowitch down. As his family ties with Romain Gary were no secret, the true identity behind the pseudonym 'Ajar' was dangerously close to being revealed. Gary had to come up with a new strategy. He decided to fictionalize elements of Pavlowitch's real life to make it more convincing that the latter was indeed the author of Ajar's writings. Not only had his fictional alter ego taken on a recognizable face, it now also gained a body. Gary produced a book with the title *Pseudo*, which posed as Ajar's autobiography. It portrayed Pavlowitch/Ajar as mentally ill, and featured his struggles during psychiatric treatment in Copenhagen. This strategy appeared to work, it convinced the readers of Ajar's authenticity. The trope of the mad artist never fails! The real, perfectly sane Pavlowitch was deeply offended, but he continued to play his role, for which he earned a decent salary. Mind you, he was not doing it for free. Seven months after Romain Gary's suicide in December 1980, the truth was uncovered when Pavlowitch published his account of the charade and appeared on Bernard Pivot's famous TV talk show *Apostrophes*.

AG: You seem to have a special interest in projects of a distinctly deceptive nature. Don't you find that there are moral questions to be asked?

LV: Today, we might call Gary's insane endeavour a durational performance of great intricacy and see it as a beautiful example of what Carrie Lambert-Beatty has described as 'parafiction'.[25] Lambert-Beatty offered some obvious moral objections against the fooling of the audience. But she has also come up with some arguments in defence of it. One of her ideas is that the bewildering experience of being misled can turn us into more critical spectators. I agree with that, and I think projects like these can give us a lot to learn from. I would even go so far as to say that an aspect of deception is unavoidable when someone has a truly meaningful motivation for sending an alter ego into the world.

AG: An aspect of self-deception as well, maybe?

LV: Yes, I think so, although this brings us close to the problematic interpretation of such projects as pathological. You could argue that in most cases, the artist's driving force is the hope that his fiction might in some way have an impact on reality. In order to create an aesthetically convincing deception, you have to believe in it yourself, at least a tiny bit. If this Pygmalion-like desire is not present, the poor alter ego would risk appearing arbitrary and lifeless, and wouldn't have a leg to stand on.

AG: I got the sense that in your project, you do not use the alter ego only to question authorship. It's also a way for you to think about our experience of the self, and the notion of the self as a fiction.

LV: Certainly, but do go on.

AG: In his book *The Ego Tunnel*, philosopher Thomas Metzinger argues that our notion of the self is nothing but a 'phenomenal self-model'. The only way our brain can help us perceive the world around us is by offering us an inner representation of it. Metzinger calls our brain a 'reality engine' that provides a sort of interface between our organism and the world.[26] We can know the world only as a virtual reality experience. In that reality, the idea of the self or the ego is the central, but entirely fictional, element.[27]

LV: Yes, our mind is constantly fooling us. We love being fooled!

AG: Furthermore, our talent for creating illusions seems to be the very thing that enabled us to advance as a species.

LV: How is that?

AG: Metzinger writes that humankind's ability to use increasingly complex tools depended on our ability to expand our 'self-model' with things external to it–the ability to integrate foreign elements into the self-model. So, this crucial step in our development was possible because we were incredibly agile in moulding the image of our bodily selves. We are masters in creating the illusion of an extended self to help us achieve our goals in life. We could use the idea of the extended self as another metaphor to think about the alter ego.

LV: Sounds interesting. That could open up a whole range of interpretations. Would you integrate that in your lecture about me? I'd be curious to see it.

[The] challenge is not only to be vigilantly skeptical... In the ocean of data we dip into to resolve both looming decisions and passing inquiries (and of course, to investigate parafictions themselves) the problem may be less how to remember to be skeptical, than how to decide when one has been sufficiently so... When does one decide that something is–in the epistemologists' phrase now codified as Wikipedia's primary criterion–*true enough?*
Carrie Lambert-Beatty[28]

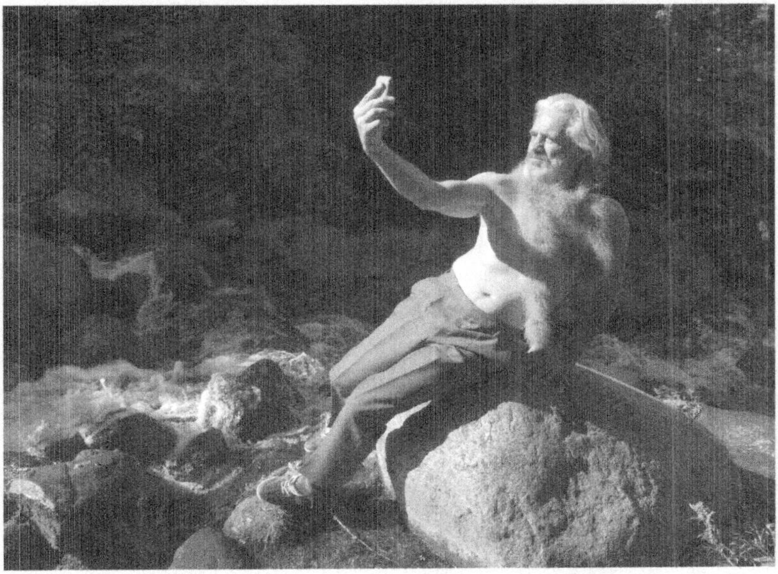

Portrait Ludovik Vermeersch © Anna Ernst

Notes

1 Quoted in Hyun Ae Lee, *'Aber ich stelle doch nochmals einen neuen Kirchner auf': Ernst Ludwig Kirchners Davoser Spätwerk* (Münster: Waxman Verlag, 2008), p. 39. Author's translation.

2 Kirchner's high hopes came true: between 1920 and 1933 this 'French poet' (his name is Louis de Marsalle) was to write six articles on the artist's work. All of them enthusiastically sing Kirchner's praises. When too many friends and colleagues started expressing the desire to get to know his unconditional supporter, Kirchner declared him dead in 1933. He had run out of excuses to explain why his non-existent friend wasn't able to meet up. Surely, Kirchner was not the only one to ever use the deceit of the fake review as an instrument for self-promotion, but there's something sad and crooked about his scheme, particularly as it involved fooling his friends, colleagues and well-meaning patrons (museum director Ernst Gosebruch was already supportive of Kirchner's work and didn't actually need convincing).

3 Roland Barthes, 'The Death of the Author', in *Image Music Text*, trans. by Stephan Heath (London: Fontana Press, 1977), p. 143.

4 Vermeersch's lecture performance was programmed on the last day of the exhibition 'My Abstract World' at collector Thomas Olbricht's private museum. This exhibition featured a selection of abstract paintings from Olbricht's collection.

5 A first version of Gorki's lecture was presented in a seminar at ARIA, Antwerp, on 9 March 2018, under the title *The Case of the Ridiculous Curator or How Transfigurative Recontextualisations May Reveal Authentic Truths.* A second, more extended version was shown on 24 June 2018 during the festival '48 Stunden Neukölln' in Berlin. Adopting Vermeersch's own habit of resorting to the figure of the alter ego, Gorki performed both lectures under a pseudonym, using the name Toon Leën.

6 This question also features as the title of the introduction to Vermeersch's publication *Personally, I'm Most Interested in the Shapes and Colours.* See Zoë De Luca and Emily Doucet, 'Who is Ludovik Vermeersch: An Introduction' in idem (Ghent: MER Paper Kunsthalle, 2015), pp. 6-9.

7 The following conversation possibly took place in the first half of November 2017 in Berlin.

8 Boris Groys, *Art Power* (Cambridge, MA: MIT Press, 2008), pp. 50-51.

9 Ibid., p. 50.

10 Ibid., p. 96.

11 Ludovik Vermeersch, 'The Work and the Discontentment of Marc Bergson', in *Personally, I'm Most Interested in the Shapes and Colours*, pp. 183, 189.

12 Sarah Thornton, *33 Artists in 3 Acts* (London: Granta, 2015).

13 Otto Rank, *Der Künstler* (Leipzig/Vienna/Zurich: Internationaler Psychoanalytischer Verlag, 1925), p. 69.

14 See also: Catherine M. Soussloff, *The Absolute Artist: The Historiography of a Concept* (Minneapolis) and London: University of Minnesota Press, 1997), pp. 115-126.

15 What Pierre Bourdieu called the 'charismatic ideology' is essentially a variation on the concept of the personality cult, that emerges with the invention of the artist biography in the Renaissance. The prototype of this new genre was Giorgio Vasari's *Vite*, or *The Lives of the Most Excellent Painters, Sculptors, and Architects* (first published in 1550), in which the artists are praised to the skies and given a quasi-divine status. Later came the secularized format of the genius, and, in the twentieth century, the radical innovator, the avant-gardist, the troublemaker appeared on the scene. Bourdieu's notion of a charismatic ideology holds that the attention is directed to 'the apparent exclusive producer... the "author", suppressing the question of what authorizes the author, what creates the authority with which authors authorize'. This fiction is maintained by all those involved. The field of art is arranged such that everything is constantly in motion to emphasize, recognize, and celebrate the authorship and the originality of the individual artist. Because the emphasis on its uniqueness is what augments the economic value of the artwork, it is clear that the art market has an enormous stake in maintaining the belief in the charismatic ideology. See Pierre Bourdieu, 'La production de la croyance', *Actes de la Recherche en Sciences Sociales* 13 (February 1977), pp. 3-43 and Ernst Kris, *Die ästhetische Illusion* (Frankfurt am

Main: Suhrkamp Verlag, 1977), p. 68.

16 In his 2016 lecture *The Ego Trip and the Research Pill*, Vermeersch argues that a narcissistic fixation pervades even the literature about the institutionalization of research in the arts. It is a common line of thinking among many advocates of this recent category that the arts should retain an exceptional position within academia. Artistic research is then defined by its subjective singularity and said to stand apart from all the other existing forms of research. A contrasting position is taken by Bert Taken and Jeroen Boomgaard in 'Art Education in a Mediatized World', in James Elkins, ed., *What Do Artists Know?* (University Park: The Pennsylvania State University Press, 2012). They argue that 'the visual arts can no longer lay claim to a domain of their own' and the artist should adopt the role of 'specialist and stakeholder' in our contemporary visual culture (see pp. 131, 132). But once you have stripped bare artists of every remaining particle of romanticism and disrobed them of the charm of uniqueness, will there be anything left that is of interest to us?

17 Thornton, *33 Artists in 3 Acts*, p. 19. The quote is taken from a chapter on Jeff Koons.

18 Ludovik Vermeersch, 'De vergeefse ontsnapping uit het ik', *FORUM⁺ voor onderzoek en kunsten/for research and arts*, herfst 2016, pp. 8–18, https://www.forum-online.be/nummers/november-2016/vergeefse-ontsnapping-uit-het-ik.

19 Joe Scanlan initially invented Woolford's character to create a different context for a group of wooden collages that he thought didn't fit his own oeuvre very well. (See Jeremy Sigler's interview with Joe Scanlan in *Bomb Magazine* 112 [1 July 2010]). Woolford was designed as an African-American woman who was younger than Scanlan and had supposedly been his studio assistant. She was played by three different actresses at exhibition openings and various performances over the years. In 2014, Woolford was included in the Whitney Biennial with a reenactment of a 1977 stand-up routine by the black comedian Richard Pryor. The artist group Yams Collective withdrew their work from the exhibition in protest: the gesture of an established white male artist disguising as a black woman at an exhibition in which black artists were underrepresented, felt as an unacceptable form of cultural appropriation. They charged against his 'conceptual rape' of the black body. In the commotion on social media that quickly followed, Scanlan's strategy was often likened to the practice of blackface minstrelsy. A self-portrait from 2002, for which he posed with dirt on his face, often accompanied this accusation. His attempted escape from the self, if you will, had now directly led him to a renewed confrontation with his own face, muddied at that.

20 Martin Doll, *Fälschung und Fake: Zur diskurskritischen Dimension des Täuschens* (Berlin: Kulturverlag Kadmos, 2012), pp. 219–222.

21 Michael Heyward, *The Ern Malley Affair* (London: Faber and Faber, 2003 [1993]), XXIV.

22 Romain Gary, *Vie et mort d'Émile Ajar*, in *Légendes du je* (Paris: Éditions Gallimard, 2009), p. 1410. This sentence is hard to translate. Gary bemoans a loss of control over his own image, as it was increasingly being defined by the outside world.

23 Ibid., p. 1411.

24 Paul Pavlowitch, *L'homme que l'on croyait* (Paris: Fayard, 1981), pp. 106–109.

25 Carrie Lambert-Beatty, 'Make-Believe: Parafiction and Plausibility', *October* 129 (Summer 2009), pp. 51–84.

26 Thomas Metzinger, *Der Ego-Tunnel* (Munich: Piper Taschenbuch, 2014), p. 40.

27 Ibid., e.g., pp. 162, 179.

28 Lambert-Beatty, 'Make-Believe', pp. 77–78.

29 The authors wish to thank Carolin Nüser for an inspiring slip of the pen and Ying Sze Pek for her helpful comments. Any remaining falsities are entirely the authors' responsibility.

Part 3

Imagining the Future

Between Realities #Athens
The Re-imagination of Public Space

Sigrid Merx

Since 2014, Platform-Scenography (P-S) organizes and curates so-called 'live action research events', in which participants are invited to actively explore and map particular public spaces from the perspective of scenography. In these events, scenographic concepts and scenographic strategies are used to challenge participants to look at familiar urban spaces in a new way, to discover new or forgotten realities and eventually, and hopefully, become aware of P-S' potentiality. Much like how in theatre the scenographer designs the actual theatre space in such a way that it allows for new possible worlds to materialize, P-S tries to curate their live action research events in such a way that in the actual material manifestation of public space, new possible manifestations can become perceptible and spaces become charged with new imaginations and possibilities.

In this contribution, I will analyze how P-S tries to establish a particular relationship between real and imaginative spaces through its live action research events. I will do so by focusing on a specific project, 'Between Realities #Athens', a 5-day live action research event that took place in 2016, in which a group of local participants explored and mapped public spaces in Athens from the point of view of 'stages of crisis'. As a member of P-S and one of the curators of this project, I will be talking from the subjective perspective of the insider. This article is a first attempt to grasp our way of working and the intentions and assumptions that support it. I will pay attention to the strategies we use, the kind of effects these evoke, and start to find the right words and concepts to critically describe and reflect on a method that is neither fixed nor finished, and that has been developed and still is developing in and through our activities.

It is not the aim of this contribution to contextualize our strategies historically or theoretically. Although such framing could definitely be interesting and valuable–for example, how does our way of working relate to the artistic interventions in public space of the Situationists or to Henri Lefebvre's theory of the production of space–it would entail a framing after the fact. These theoretical or historical references did not play a role in the development of our project at the time. And our interest now is not so much to establish a context *around* our work, but rather to unfold our work from *within*, and to describe and analyze as precisely and accurately as possible our methodology, which up till this point has remained rather implicit and intuitive and is, as we believe, worth unpacking.

Platform-Scenography's Take on Scenography

Platform-Scenography is a Dutch platform of scenographers and dramaturgs interested in the question of how spaces work both in and outside the theatre, and how, in their specific material manifestation, structural organization, and locatedness, they produce and facilitate potential actions and experiences.[1] We are not interested in what a space might represent or mean, but how it performs. What does the space do? What does it do to us, how does it affect us? What does it allow us to do in it and with it? And how does it do that? And, most importantly, P-S wants to find out what spaces do and how they perform, not by thinking *about* these spaces, but thinking *in*, *with* and *through* them; by going into the spaces we want to explore, to observe, and to map them carefully, preferably with others, because *thinking space* for P-S is a collective practice that benefits from a multiplicity of perspectives, experiences, and knowledges. For this aim, P-S organizes and curates live action research events, a form of what I call 'scenographic mapping', in which public spaces are collectively explored in situ and observations and findings are shared and, preferably, made public.

Our focus in the process of mapping is not so much on the end result, that is, a map, but on mapping as a process. Ideally, we also share this process with a public who is not directly participating in the event, making visible the research process and the continuing accumulation of observations, results, and findings. This coming into being of a—never finished or final—map during the research can be presented in an offline (exhibition) space, but also online, for example on a website. By making the research visible as it unfolds, we stress both the performativity and the processual nature of mapping as research, as something that produces knowledge in its doing. Finally, characteristic of our live research events is that we not only explore and map public spaces, but also intervene in them in some way. Therefore, an element of intervention is always somehow present in our events. By doing this, we want to stress that (public) space is not fixed, but unfolds in time. It comes into being through what we do in it and how we engage with it. In other words, space is not a given, and can be actively negotiated and re-negotiated, imagined and re-imagined.

Expanding Scenography

Platform-Scenography's understanding of and approach towards scenography can be located in the practical field of what is sometimes called 'expanding scenography'. In a more traditional understanding, scenography has long been associated with the design of settings for the performance of dramatic works on stage. However, as editors Joslin McKinney and Scott Palmer mention in their introduction to *Scenography Expanded: An Introduction to Contemporary Performance Design*, the notion of scenography has expanded drastically, and 'the capacity for scenography to operate independently from a theatre text ... as the central component of a performance, not merely as a backdrop to a play, is now widely in evidence'.[2]

As Sodja Lotker and Richard Gough suggest in a special issue of *Performance Research* on scenography, scenography can happen anywhere, in 'our home, a restaurant, a cruise ship, a parking lot, a public square, a theatre venue, a parliamentary building and Everest'.[3] Lotker and Gough stress that scenography can both be built (by a scenographer, a collective of artists, an architect, or nature itself) and found (by an actor, a dancer, or spectator).[4] Continuing Lotker's and Gough's vocabulary, P-S can be described as a collective of scenographers and dramaturgs that on the one hand is interested in scenographies found outside the theatre, and on the other hand builds an environment in which the research event can take place, in order to collectively investigate these scenographies.

Expanding scenography entails a non-presentational understanding of scenography which, as McKinney and Scott Palmer claim, allows to foreground scenography 'as a mode of encounter and exchange, founded on spatial and material relations between bodies, objects, and environments', and, as a result, shifts the attention from the designer to those who experience these relations.[5] When we indeed approach scenography as a mode of encounter and exchange, we can start to see how P-S' live research events are a form of scenography, in the sense that they entail curated encounters and exchanges between participants, objects, and public environments. The question is, what precisely is scenographic about this kind of curation? Or, to put it differently, how can we characterize the scenographic qualities of P-S' practice? And, in the context of this article, how do these scenographic qualities then contribute to the establishment of a particular relation between real and imagined spaces?

McKinney and Palmer identify three interrelated concepts that they use to describe the core principles of so-called 'expanded scenography' and that are very suitable to describe how P-S understands scenography and tries to put those principles to use. First, *relationality* points to how scenography facilitates spatial encounters, and positions and repositions subjects and objects in an environment. This process of positioning and repositioning often implies a shift of perspective on and a 'new' experience of familiar spaces, and potentially gives way to the active re-imagining of existing social structures.[6] Second, *affectivity* describes how scenography appeals to the whole body of the spectator and invites the attention of the spectator through experience. As a result, meaning and understanding are generated through the sensual, emotional, and aesthetic responses on the part of the spectator. Scenography offers a set of experiential potentialities rather than a singular message that needs to be decoded. Affectivity also emphasizes the processual nature of the scenographic experience. The scenographic experience gradually unfolds in time and space, accumulating associations and meanings.[7] Third, *materiality* explains how scenography enters the spectators into a material composition, in which they are not only brought into direct contact with both human and non-human materials, but also are acknowledged as a material in their own right.[8] Their physical presence, energy, attention, and responses, as already mentioned with respect to the concept of affectivity, are part of the scenography. Scenography recognizes materiality as an important force in producing spatial affect.[9]

Liesbeth Groot Nibbelink, in her article 'How does scenography think?', suggests to add a fourth concept to McKinney's and Palmer's framework, namely *temporality*.[10] Although McKinney and Palmer do refer to the processual nature of performance, Groot Nibbelink argues for a more particular scenographic understanding of temporality. Temporality, in her account, deals with how spaces materialize in time, change over time, and how time leaves its traces in space. Scenography can play with and use this spatiotemporal dynamic. Moreover, Groot Nibbelink suggests, scenography can function as a spatial script or scenario for potential actions: 'Spaces are deeply procedural, they generate behaviour and define how once executes procedures ...'.[11] Precisely these actions and behaviours, be it by performers or spectators, change space and make it appear and perform in a particular way.

I believe *potentiality*, although implied in and therefore partly overlapping with McKinney's and Palmers' discussion of relationality and affectivity and Groot Nibbelink's understanding of temporality, is worth being emphasized even more within this conceptual framework–particularly when we want to describe and understand how in expanded scenography in general, and in P-S' work in public space in particular, the real and the imaginative relate to one another. Potentiality, then, in my understanding, points not only to how scenography creates the spatial conditions for potential experiences (see McKinney and Palmer) and actions (see Groot Nibbelink), but how, through creating those conditions, it also calls potential spaces into being; spaces that are there but have not manifested themselves yet, ready to unfold and to be unfolded in the actions and experiences of performers and spectators. Obviously, the relation between physically present space and imagined space lies at the heart of scenography as theatrical practice. Scenography, as also Groot Nibbelink points out in her article, by nature deals with the design of relations between on- and offstage, between presentation and representation, between physical space and fictional space.

With the conceptual framework now in place, let's turn our attention to 'Between Realities # Athens'. Before I start analyzing our project in the light of the abovementioned principles and address how P-S uses scenography to point to the possibility of reimagining existing spaces, I will introduce and describe the project more carefully, to allow the reader to form a more precise idea of what happened during this five-day live action research event.

Between Realities #Athens

The research event, which took place in Athens in October 2016, was commissioned by Thanos Vovolis, scenographer and curator of the exhibition '[OUT] TOPIAS: Performance and Public/Outdoor Space' in the Benaki Museum in Athens. The exhibition focused on the political and social dimensions of public space as performance space. Participants in our live action research event had responded to an Open Call that had been distributed in local networks of designers, scenographers, and architects. It invited people to explore the city of Athens with us through the conceptual framework of 'stages of crisis'. Nine young, local, and because of the economic crisis mostly unemployed professionals signed up for the event. The group was a mix of costume designers, set designers, architects, urban planners, and art historians. The home base for our event was an exposition room in the Benaki Museum, where observations and findings were collected, processed, and exhibited on the go, in a slowly growing and ever-changing exhibition open to the public. For this project, P-S worked together with WE-ARE-AMP, a creative studio by Moniek Ellen and Tim Heijmans that explores the boundaries between traditional graphic techniques, spatial design, new media, and web design.

Framing Athens as a city in and of crisis was an important conceptual starting point for the event, as we suggested to explore actual stages of crisis in the city. This particular framing allowed us to introduce our scenographic perspective to analyze stages and acts of staging outside the theatre. Not only did we frame the space of our investigation in a particular way, we also framed ourselves in a particular role. We presented ourselves as 'cultural pilgrims', travelling to Athens 'to get infected by real engagement and revolt',[12] alluding to the increasing tendency of West-European artists and curators to go to Athens. Athens, where it supposedly is all happening, and where, because of the crisis and lack of funding, the arts (that is at least often the assumption) dare to be critical, resistant, non-institutional, and engaged. Athens, where you can feel that art is still alive and something is somehow at stake. We played with the (misplaced) romantic appeal of a crisis that is not ours; an appeal we admittedly also felt ourselves. We made a video clip that we sent to the participants and which was exhibited in the museum before our actual arrival, expressing our understanding of Athens as a city of crisis. Using all kinds of audio-visual material from the Internet, the video provided a deliberately one-dimensional, stereotypical image of Athens as a city of constant demonstrations and riots, xenophobia, local soup kitchens, and homeless immigrants, with the famous Syntagma Square featuring prominently as the absolute stage of crisis.

On the first day of the research event, we persisted in our problematic frame. Although new to the city, we staged ourselves as experts with knowledge and brought the group to Syntagma Square in front of the Greek parliament, which we presented as the iconic stage of crisis in Athens. We introduced the group to our scenographic perspective of observing and analyzing public space, and started to explore the square collectively, paying close attention to the interaction of bodies, objects, and the environment. Participants were invited to document their observations with pictures, sketches, notes, and sound recordings that were incorporated into the museum exhibition space. We discussed how in particular the scenography of the square may have supported previous 'scenes of crisis' and how it might produce future ones. In these discussions the participants, as we had anticipated and hoped, pointed out to us that according to them Syntagma Square was not the real stage of crisis and that we had brought them to the wrong place. They felt other places in Athens could serve as better examples of how the crisis (had) manifested itself in the city.

On the second day, we switched roles drastically. We invited the participants to be the experts and to guide us in small groups to alternative locations of crisis in the city. This resulted in four walks through the city, taking us into different directions. I will briefly describe three of these walks. One group brought us to one of the many covered shopping arcades that are nestled in the historical buildings in the city centre. Traditionally, this particular arcade was filled with many independent little bookshops, a true Walhalla for Athenian book lovers and a hidden centre of intellectual life; but since the economic crisis the shops had been forced to shut down one by one, leaving them vacated and turning the alley into a ghostly area. Another group took us to one of the university campus and presented it to us as the control room of many political demonstrations and protests. The walls of the campus were completely covered with political slogans and images. Being a student in Athens, the group explained, almost automatically implies being politically engaged and active, and students play a crucial role in the organization of all kinds of protest. A third group took us on what they called 'a bloody tour of deathly violence'. They respectively guided us to the anarchistic district Exarcheia, where in December 2008 Alexandros Grigoropoulous, a 15-year-old Greek student was killed by two police officers, resulting in large protests and demonstrations, which escalated to widespread rioting, and to Stadiou Street, the main street used for protests and demonstrations, where in May 2010 three bank employees were killed as protesters set fire to the Marfin Bank (located on that street) during a general strike over planned austerity measures. The often very intimate and personal stories the participants told us on these walks were tales full of anger, frustration, pain, and loss. We realized we knew nothing of crisis.

On the third day, we tried to challenge the participants to let go of the position of personally involved insider and to try for a moment not to look at these spaces as bearers of (tragic) histories, but as a particular form of scenography. We introduced a more elaborate conceptual framework with which to analyze these locations, using the traditional spatial distinction between stage, backstage, wings, and auditorium as our starting point. Collectively we defined particular (energetic) qualities and characteristics for each of these aspects of theatre space. These characteristics, and the qualities associated with them, were meant to function as a legend, enabling the participants to map and explore the spaces they had selected from this particular spatial perspective, and to see where stage, backstage, wings, and auditorium could be located in public space, where the boundaries between them could be found, and how their relations were organized.[13]

Being sent back into the city, this time not as deeply involved local citizens but as scenographic explorers who try to map and document a space, had an interesting impact on many of the participants, even though many struggled with applying the conceptual framework to the actual space. The shift of frame prompted at least some of the groups to look at their selected stages of crisis in a new way. For example, the group that was investigating the empty shopping arcade started to address the notion of an empty stage as not necessarily a negative value. Instead of looking at the space merely as a depressive symptom of decline and economic crisis, they tried to imagine the shopping arcade as a performance environment, literally an empty stage where something new could happen. In their further documentation of the space they now started to focus on the performative potential of the space, imagining what was there to be seen for a potential audience, thinking about how an audience might be positioned in and guided through this space in order to see the space 'perform'. And although this did not change the material manifestation of the space as such, nor did it solve the problem of vacated shops, it did change the disposition of the participants towards the space: they started to see and understand that the space could be seen in a different, less negative, light.

In the group that had focused on sites of violence, something different happened. Although the framework–stage, backstage, wings, auditorium–was not productive for them in revisiting the locations and they soon decided to let go of it, they did feel triggered to try to look at these locations more from the perspective of space itself, instead of from the more personal, emotional, and historical point of view. Looking back at their documentation of the previous day, they noticed they felt most attracted to some close-up images they had made. Somewhat intuitively they realized that these images helped them to get rid of what one of the participants called 'the burden of history'. They also liked the abstract aesthetics of these close-up images and how it reduced the space to line, form, colour, and material. Therefore, they decided to continue using the close-up as a strategy to map their spaces. They attempted to transform the space into an abstract image beyond concrete geographical and historical recognition, and to show its inherent beauty beyond the blood that had been shed in it.

Finally, on the fourth and the fifth day, we asked the groups to create an alternative city tour for local citizens and tourists, based on their new perspective on the spaces they had explored. Each group physically marked their tour in the city with stickers and created a small guide with image, text, and instructions for potential audiences of the tour. The guide could be printed on demand in the exhibition room by the visitors. The aim of the alternative city guides was to share these new perspectives on locations in the city with a wider public and to create a kind of meaningful 'afterlife' for our research. Unfortunately, as far as we know, no visitor printed a guide and went on a tour; for that matter, the city guides died a quiet death. In a way, so did the exhibition itself once we left Athens and were no longer present in the museum to explain our research and its development to occasional visitors. The main problem, it seemed, and we had struggled with this before in previous similar projects, was the illegibility of the project for those who did not directly participate in it. This raises the question of whether the project has a value and impact that stretches beyond the event itself and the personal experiences of its direct participants. Related to this is the question of whether it is a problem when the 'meaning' of an event resides in these personal, but shared, experiences and if it is relevant or not to try to communicate these with others. We, as Platform-Scenography, are constantly struggling with these questions and haven't come to a definite answer.

In spite of these difficulties, what did make this research event valuable, as far as I am concerned, is how it fostered the possibility of reimagining public space. By radically reframing the spaces they mapped, the participants imagined these real, existing spaces as something else or more than stages of and for crisis. Re-imagination, in this respect, also turned out to be an act of re-appropriation; it entailed reclaiming public space from the limiting and paralyzing narrative of crisis and quite literally suggesting a different perspective from which to look at the space, which seemed to give some participants at least a sense of potential agency. In the last part of this article I will analyze in a more systematic way how this effect was achieved. What strategies can we distinguish that enabled this effect? In what way are these strategies scenographic? For this, I will use the previously discussed core concepts of expanded scenography as my framework: relationality, affectivity, materiality, temporality, and potentiality.

Scenographic Strategies for Reimagining Public Space

To look at familiar spaces in a new way requires looking beyond what we have come to believe is there. In order to see and experience what else is there, we need, to a certain extent, to 'undo' our experience and knowledge. With this research event P-S deliberately played with the notion of *knowing* Athens. Different kinds of knowledge were addressed. First, mediatized knowledge: knowing the city through its representations in the media. The clip with a one-dimensional depiction of Athens as a city in crisis with which the project started represented this type of knowledge. Second, personal and situated knowledge: knowing the city because you live and work there, because memories and experiences have been formed there. This knowledge was embodied by every participant. The event was designed in such a way that it could facilitate the destabilization of prior knowledge. By inviting the participants to guide us through the city, they were able to undo our one-dimensional, Western-European, quasi-romantic understanding of the city as we had presented it in our video and on the first day of the event, showing us new stages and new perspectives. But also, the situated knowledge of our participants was undone, as the project challenged them to let go of their personal knowledge of the city and to engage with these familiar places in a different way and from a different perspective. It was very interesting to see how at a certain point in the process the dominant frame of understanding Athens as a city of crisis, a frame that not only the media, or we as Platform-Scenography, but also the participants with their personal stories had helped maintain, was deliberately overthrown by the group to make room for different understandings and imaginations. How could this happen?

If we indeed approach scenography as a mode of spatial encounter (relationality), the question is how 'Between Realities...' created the spatial conditions in which the participants could engage with the city in such a way that a new experience of that city became possible. Or, to use once more Groot Nibbelink's words, how did the scenography of the event create a spatial scenario for the participants to act in the city and to produce new meanings? What procedures were put in place? I suggest the following three, closely related, strategies played a crucial role: the multiplication of the stage, the repositioning of the participant, and the organization of research as an event.

Multiplication of the stage points to the fact that we made the space we explored explode from one central stage of crisis, Syntagma Square, into a series of stages scattered around the city. Concretely, we started collectively investigating one specific place that we had predetermined as the iconic stage of crisis, only to use it as a springboard to challenge the participants to locate and map other stages of crisis elsewhere, based on their knowledge, experience, and personal interests, and to invite them to present and share these locations to and with others. Their reactions, responses to, and actions in the spaces were considered integral to the research, acknowledging the presence of the participants as a material in itself (materiality). The scenography of the event was focused on creating the conditions to be open to such responses, to accommodate them, and to be affected by them (affectivity).

Repositioning the participant is closely related to the multiplication of the stage as it pertains to the constantly changing positions of the participants in and between the spaces under investigation (relationality). This mobility not only entailed going in and out the museum and into the city every day, or going from one particular stage of crisis in the city to another, but also revisiting the same locations over the course of days. Accompanying this physical mobility was what I would like to call a 'mental' mobility. Throughout the event participants were confronted with shifting roles and frames. We addressed them both as pupil and expert, as personally involved citizen and scenographic researcher. We provoked them with simplifications about their city and challenged them to show us the real Athens. We invited them to share their personal stories about the places they took us to and we asked them to observe these spaces from a conceptual framework. Both these spatial and mental shifts asked for a constant renegotiation with the actual spaces and situation on the part of the participants. Important to stress is that, because the participants were constantly positioned *in* the spaces they had to engage with, these negotiations were not merely theoretical or conceptual, but played out on an embodied and affective level, allowing the participants not only to discuss, but also to experience the complexity, multiplicity, and transformability of space (affectivity). Both the multiplication of the stage and the repositioning of the participant entailed a form of destabilization that undermined the idea of a stable situation, stable space, or stable perspective. I believe this was a crucial and necessary condition to enable participants to shift their perspective on a familiar space towards a new experience and imagination of that space (relationality).

Another important strategy, closely related to the aforementioned spatial strategies, is the particular temporal design of 'Between Realities #Athens' which foregrounded the processual nature of research. To decide upon an event that would last five days was to allow for focusing on different perspectives on different days, for clashes to occur between those perspectives, for questions to be raised and to be left dangling in the air for the moment, for associations to be dissolved or built over time, experiences to sink in and, maybe most importantly, for awareness to grow organically. P-S calls its project a live action research *event* for a reason. Approaching research as event means research is seen as something that happens and is created in the moment. We, deliberately and consciously, created space for the gradual and organic accumulation of observations, associations, understanding, and meaning in our project (affectivity). The organizing principle for this process of accumulation, as indicated before, was friction. We tried to organize constant radical shifts. I believe that confronting participants with different spaces, different roles, and different perspectives from day to day had a profound impact on the participants and on how the event unfolded. By curating 'Between Realities #Athens' as an event we invited what Henk Borgdorff with respect to artistic research terms 'unfinished thinking'.[14] No formal knowledge, but an articulation of the pre-reflective and non-conceptual, a thinking in, through and with space.

One of the consequences of these constant shifts was also that participants often felt confused, not sure what was expected of them or what direction we were heading towards, which for some had a negative impact on their motivation to participate. Some participants left the project early. For us the most important thing was to be transparent to the participants about what we were doing and to create enough space for them to discuss the process and these uncertainties.

'Between Realities #Athens' was never meant to tell *how* spaces can or should be reimagined. Imagination is not something that can be forced. As such, the project did not aim for the design of concrete new scenarios for the city, nor was it a workshop for urban activism. In that respect, we could say that the concrete impact of this project was limited. Rather, this project, on a much more generic level, was about practicing a different kind of spatial sensitivity that might help us grasp the performative and therefore transformative nature of space; a sensitivity and awareness we believe is necessary for any kind of actual, concrete change in the city to occur. Using different strategies of destabilization, we tried to facilitate an embodied, localized, and personalized spatial awareness of the seemingly simple, but actually profound, fact that spaces *can* be reimagined. We tried to create the conditions in which the simultaneous presence of actual and virtual spaces might be experienced. We fostered possible transitions from the real to the imagined. When on the third day one group, while mapping and observing their spaces, saw the potential of the empty stage in the shopping arcade, and another group found beauty in a site of horror through the close-up image, this was no formal knowledge about the potentiality of space nor a concrete idea on how to reshape these spaces, but an emerging awareness of how real and imagined spaces co-exist, how you can see the (abstract) potential of these spaces shine right through their material presences.

This reminds me of how James Corner, in the context of cartography, defines performative mapping; a definition that, I believe, also aptly describes our scenographic approach towards mapping. Mapping, according to Corner, is an act of 'uncovering realities previously unseen or unimagined, even across seemingly exhausted grounds'.[15] Scenographic mapping operates between actual and virtual spaces, between what is there and what can be imagined. It allows participants, to use Corner's words, to un-fold potential: 'it re-makes territory over and over again, each time with new and diverse consequences'.[16]

Re-imagination Disclaimer: or How to Reclaim Imagination

In the light of the global challenges we face, such as climate change, migration, overpopulation, urbanization, polarization, and economic crises, arts and design are increasingly called upon to come up with solutions and to invest their time and expertise in innovative problem solving. More and more often we see examples of how artists and designers are invited by politicians, policy makers, and corporations to join forces in what has become a trendy slogan: re-imagining our future. In this context artists and designers are often conceived of as the bearers of imagination; the ones who dare to think out-of-the box, who are able to come up with radical alternatives, to envision different futures. Increasingly we witness how outside the arts imagination has come to be understood as a functional tool for actual problem solving and how, accordingly, art and design are expected to prove their social value by using their imagination for real solutions to real problems. In this respect, fiction and the real have become entangled in a rather problematic way. I truly believe that imagination does allow for a radical re-thinking and re-imagination of how we organize our lives, our relationships with others, and the world and environment we live in. However, we should never render imagination instrumental and reduce it to a tool, a means to a concrete, specific end, because that is precisely when imagination will lose its force.

Notes

1 www.platform-scenography.nl.
2 Joslin McKinney and Scott Palmer, eds., *Scenography Expanded: An Introduction to Contemporary Performance Design* (London: Bloomsbury Methuen Drama, 2016), p. 1.
3 Sodja Lotker and Richard Gough, 'On Scenography: Editorial', *Performance Research* 18, no. 3 (2013), p. 3.
4 Ibid., p. 3.
5 McKinney and Palmer, *Scenography Expanded*, p. 2.
6 Ibid., pp. 8–10.
7 Ibid., pp. 10–12.
8 The notion of the spectator 'entering into composition' with space is derived from Liesbeth Groot Nibbelink's theory on nomadic theatre as laid out in her doctorate *Nomadic Theatre: Staging Movement and Mobility in Contemporary Performance* (2015). Groot Nibbelink in turn was inspired by Deleuze and Guattari's theory of becoming and their notion of 'aparallel evolutions', encounters between two heterogeneous elements which in *A Thousand Plateaus* (2004) they qualify as processes of 'entering into composition' with the other (p. 289).
9 McKinney and Palmer, *Scenography Expanded*, pp. 12–13.
10 Liesbeth Groot Nibbelink, 'How does scenography think?', in *Thinking through Theatre and Performance*, eds. Maaike Bleeker et al. (London and New York: Bloomsbury, 2019).
11 Ibid.
12 'To get infected by real engagement and revolt' was part of the slogan on our poster and was also used in our promo video.
13 The logic of stage, backstage, wings and auditorium was also used for the spatial lay-out and design of the exhibition space, allowing for the systematic categorization and exhibition of the research findings.
14 Henk Borgdorff, 'The production of knowledge in artistic research', *The Routledge Companion to Research in the Arts*, eds. Henrik Karlsson and Michael Biggs (New York: Routledge, 2011), p. 44.
15 James Corner, 'The Agency of Mapping: Speculation, Critique and Invention', *Mappings*, ed. Denis Cosgrove (London: Reaktion Books, 1999), p. 213.
16 Ibid., p. 213.

(Dis)placed Interventions
Between Common and Public Space

Elly Van Eeghem

I look back at the different images of public spaces that I have photographed or collected in recent years. I re-listen to audio recordings of conversations I had with city planners, residents, architects, policy makers, community workers ... I bring this multitude of images and statements together in a book and a performance and offer a multiple view of what urbanization is and does. The quest for the public space is crucial for me. What does public mean? Where is the city a public (space)? Who is the public? How do you create publics? I am constantly searching for changing image selections to find answers to questions that concern me.

> How does the stairwell ('the common part') of a residential building relate to the street? Is public space full or empty, inside or outside?
>
> What ideas about the public transformed a park or square, initially designed as a meeting place, into a nice green area only to look at? What impact does a brilliant but never realized design plan have on the collective memory of public space?
>
> Is a city district with public transport more public than a parcelled car landscape?
>
> How do we, who organize one-day car-free 'street parties' on a motorway viaduct, differ from those who celebrated this newly opened viaduct full of faith in progress years ago?

All images circle around one essential question:

> What makes this common landscape public space?

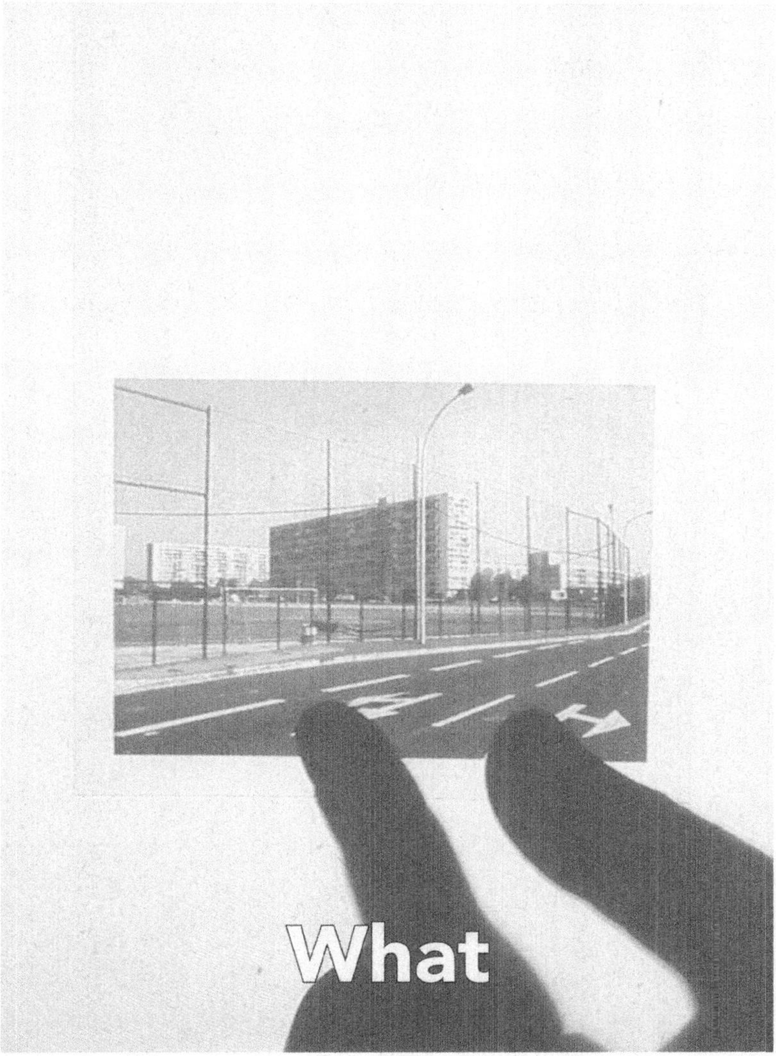
What

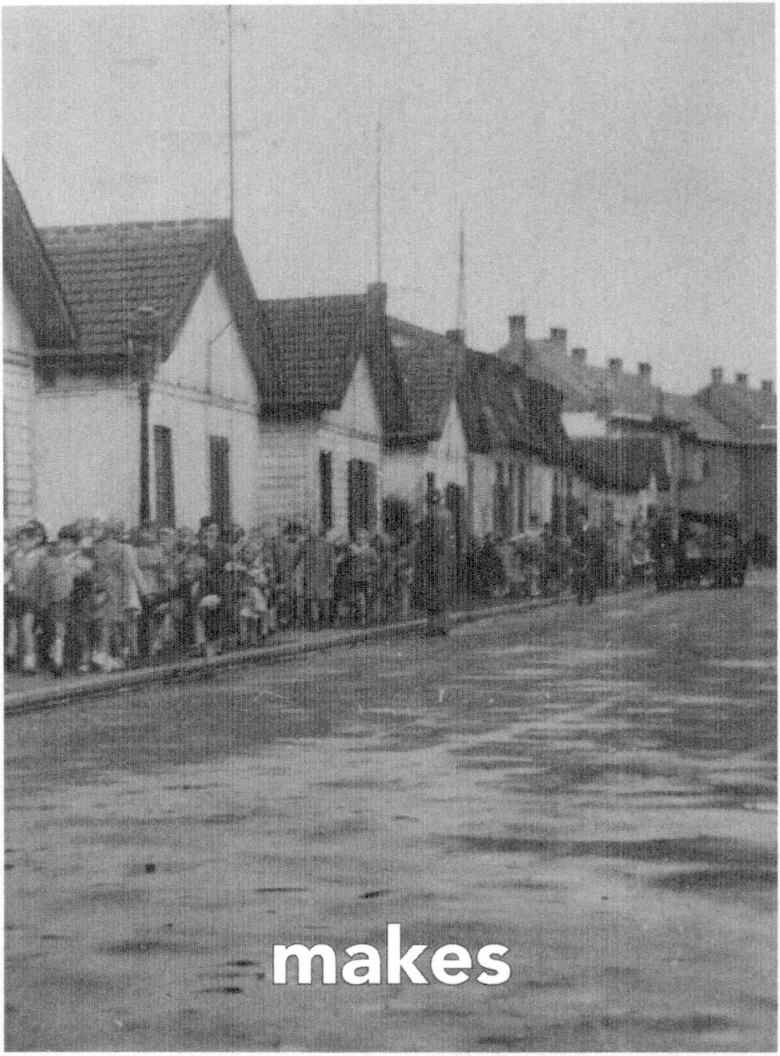
makes

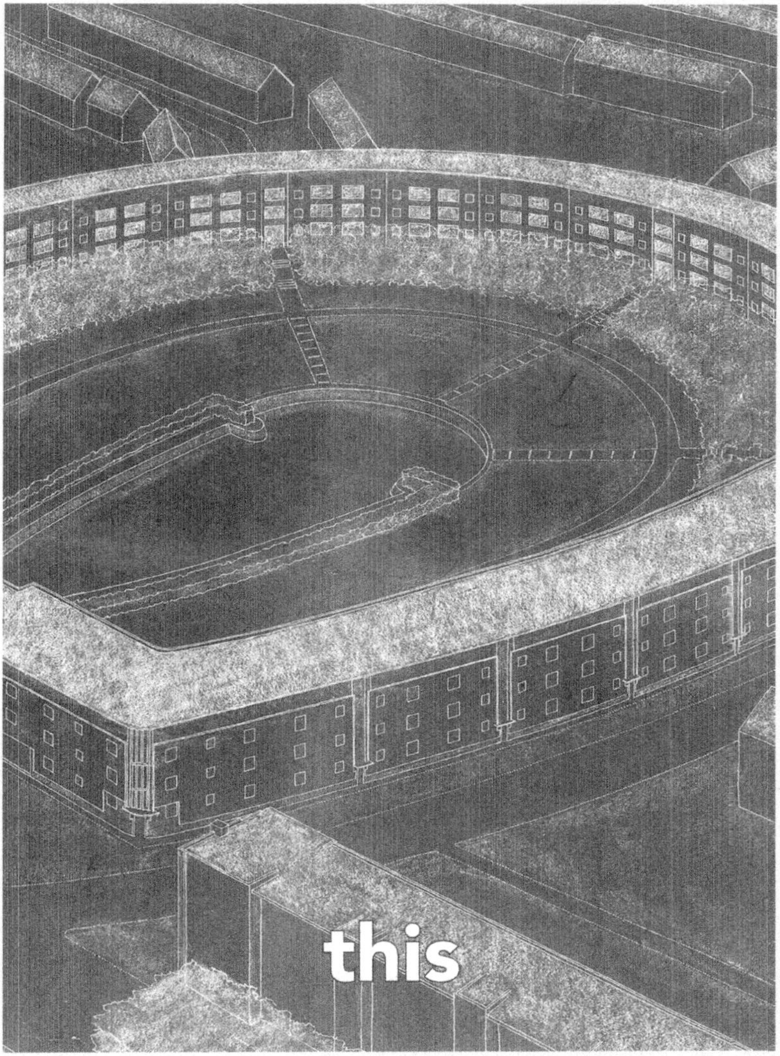
this

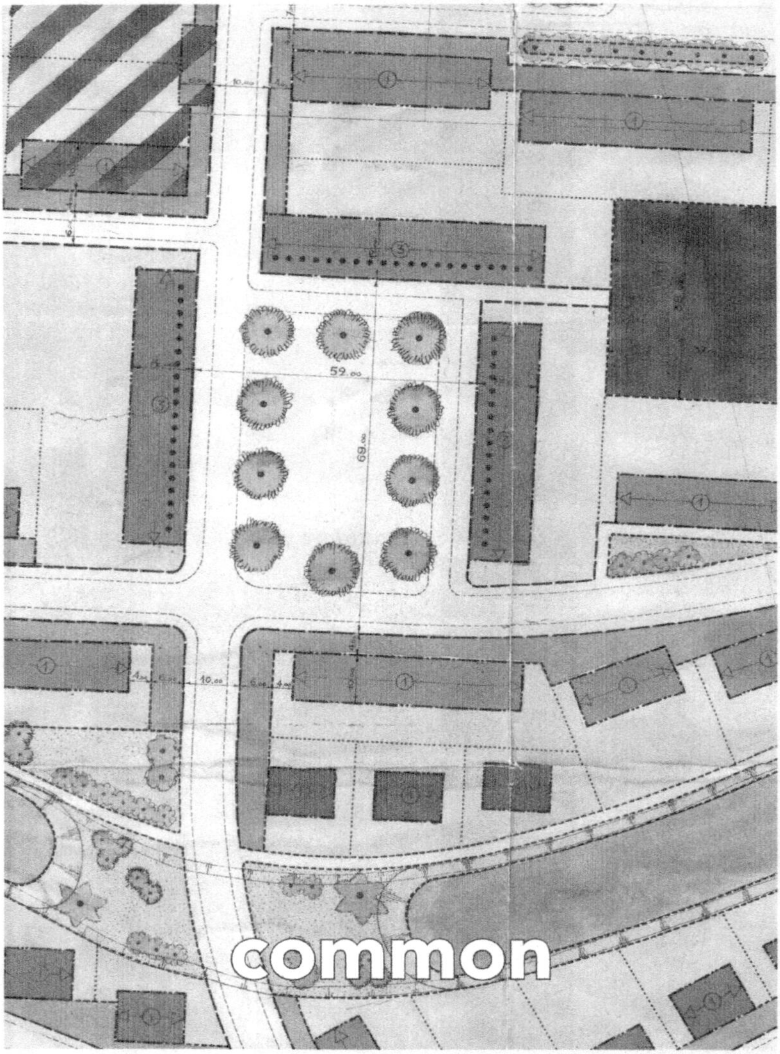
59.00
69.00
common

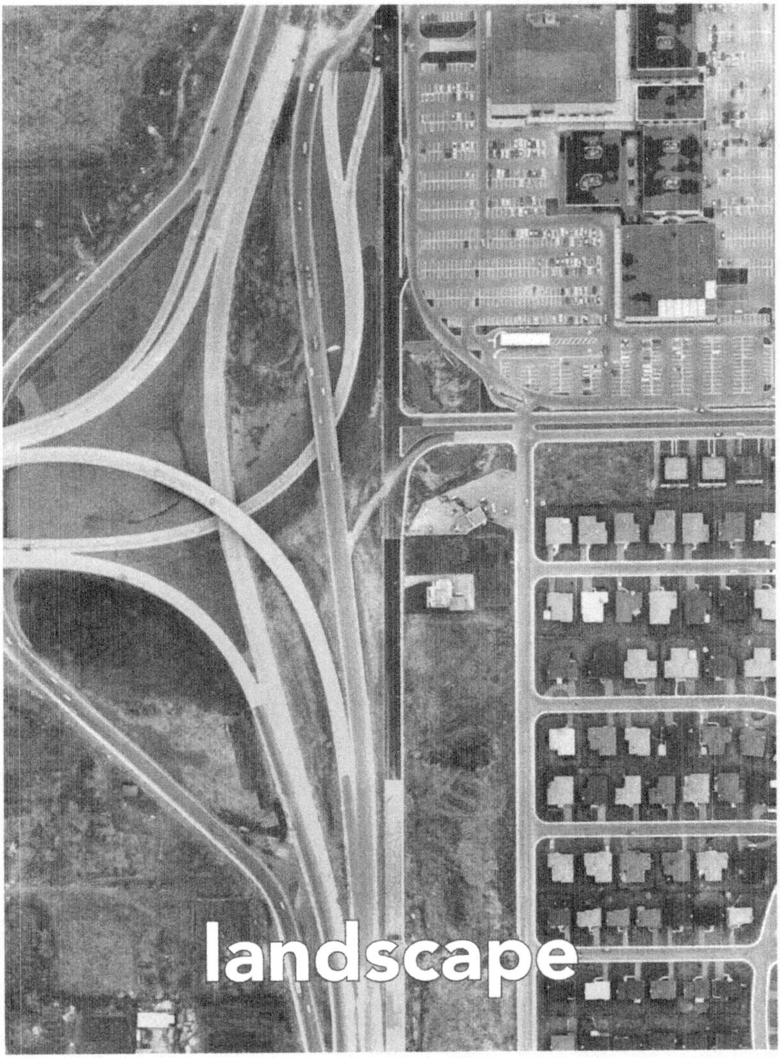
landscape

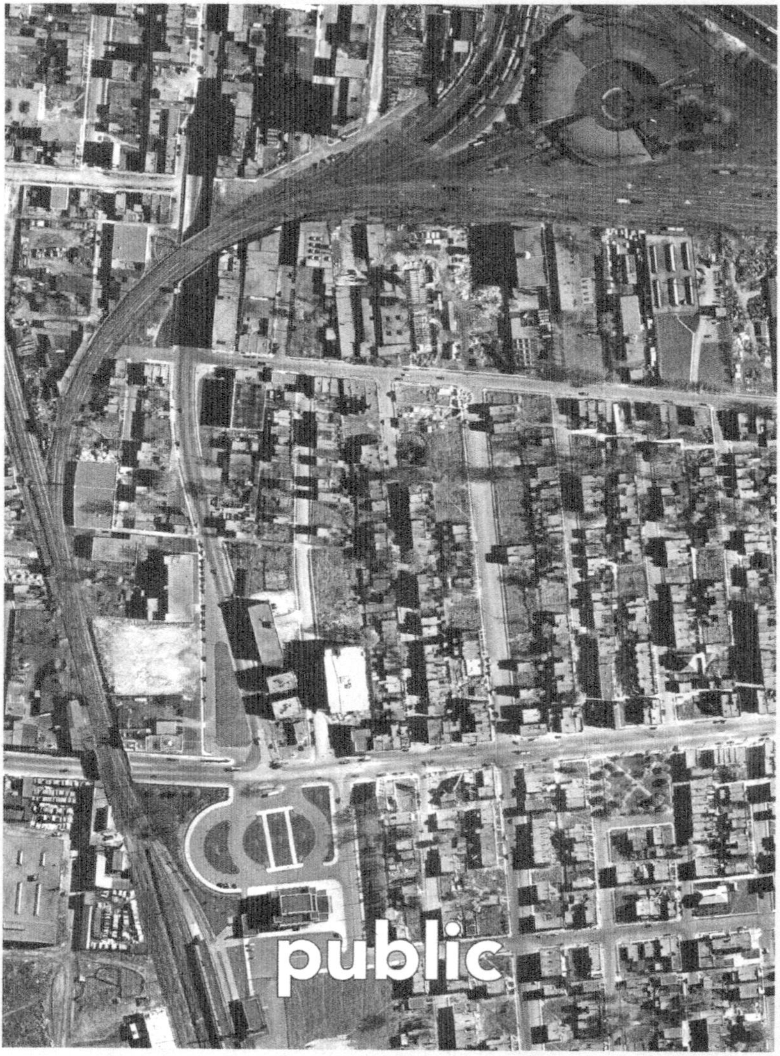
public

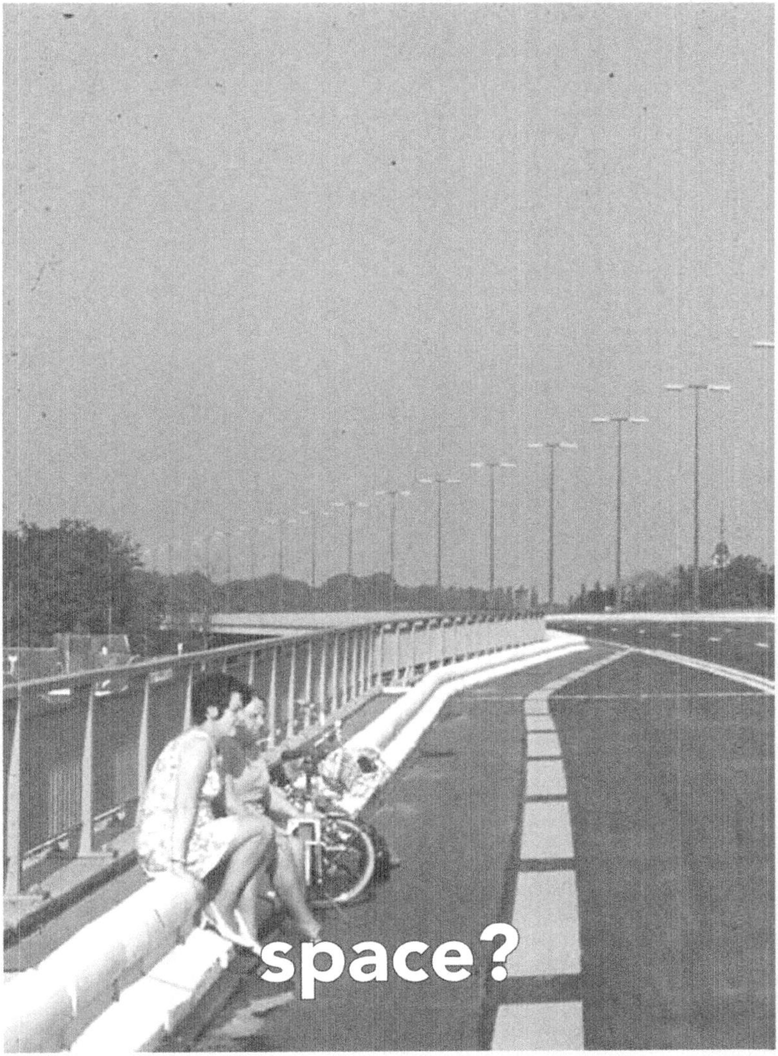
space?

Images

- *What*: street scene Asnières-sur-Seine Paris 1989 (overhead projection) © Archives Asnières
- *makes*: street scene Bloemekenswijk Ghent 1953, personal archive Elly Van Eeghem
- *this*: detail from a design drawing with a Central swimming pond at the Horseshoe Estate 1928 © Landesarchiv Berlin
- *common*: detail from the Special Planning Scheme with a central commercial square at Malem, Ghent 1951 © Ghent City Archive
- *landscape*: aerial view of the Metropolitan highway, Rockland shopping centre and the Town of Mount Royal 1959 © Archives nationales du Quebec (BAnQ)
- *public*: aerial view of Park Avenue Train Station and Park Extension, Montreal 1947 © BAnQ
- *space?*: opening of the E17 highway overpass, Ghent 1970 © Ghent City Archive

TALOS/Talos
What Sort of Future Do We Want to See Performed?

Jonas Rutgeerts,
Nienke Scholts

> And Talos, the man of bronze, ... given by the son of Cronos to Europa to be the warder of Crete and to stride round the island thrice a day with his feet of bronze. (Apollonius Rhodius, *The Argonautica*, 3rd century BC)

The performance *Talos*[1] by Arkadi Zaides took its cue from TALOS, or Transportable Autonomous Patrol for Land bOrder Surveillance, a European sponsored research and development project for which an international consortium of organizations joined forces. TALOS aspired to develop and test a mobile robotic system for border control.[2] Originally, the aim of the artistic research was to re-enact this project, taking as a starting point the actual development of a ground-drone that could detect people and prevent them from crossing a predefined border. However, the research on the European project brought to light that TALOS' goal was not confined to the construction of a robotic surveillance vehicle. The project also tried to shape our vision on the future of Europe's protection by aligning this future with Europe's mythical past. Confronted with this complexity, what was originally set up as a re-construction of a robotic vehicle soon transformed into a performance that explores the manifold temporalities that are folded into the discourse of *Talos*. Rather than referring to, or re-examining TALOS, the project here focused on Talos as an idea and on the future that this idea seems to hold. In this article we aim to elaborate on the complexities and questions that arose during the artistic process of creating *Talos*. In doing so we do not only want to come to a better understanding of the actual performance, but also outline an approach to the documentary that focuses on the creative potential of documents and shifts the perspective from re-enacting the past to pre-enacting the future. We situate this approach within a broader discourse on speculation and of a movement of activating alternative futures.

1. Talos, a Man of Bronze

The figure of Talos makes its first appearance in ancient Greek mythology. In the epic poem *The Argonautica* by Apollonius Rhodius, Talos is staged as a giant bronze automaton, a gift from Zeus to his lover Europa. Talos had the task to protect Europa against potential threats. To do this the automaton patrolled Crete, the island where Europa was staying, encircling it three times a day.[3] When intruders who wanted to harm Europa tried to reach the island, Talos threw rocks at their ships, sinking them to the bottom of the Mediterranean Sea. If intruders still made it to the shore, Talos captured them, heated up his bronze body and burned them to death.

Talos: a giant man of bronze, a robotic figure that protects Europa against intruders. Today, this description could fit an organization like Frontex, a (giant) non-human yet artificial intelligent border guard, and on a more abstract level we could even see Talos in Europe's politics of exclusion and fear. From the European perspective a helper or even hero, from an outside perspective a monster of security and control.

2. TALOS, an Autonomous Vehicle for European Border Control

In 2008 fourteen organizations, among them research institutions and universities as well as companies that were involved in communication, software development, and aviation, started working together to create an autonomous vehicle for border control: TALOS.[4] In their research and development project the 'bronze giant' is replaced by a 'fully autonomous robotic craft' that would be able to 'perform routine patrols and react to typical situations without constant human supervision'.[5] Despite the fact that the European project recycles the ancient Greek logic, the project seems to be far less effective than its Greek predecessor. Whereas the bronze giant in the Greek mythology appears as a formidable killing machine that is able to take out entire ships in the blink of an eye, the semi-autonomous vehicle that is produced by the European consortium looks like it is in no way fit to really perform its task. Although the vehicle has some resemblance to a military tank, its small size and design, a beige platform with a grass-green top and two cameras in the front that look like eyes, make it resemble Walt Disney's *Love Bug* or Pixar's *Wall-E* more than a machine that is designed for confrontational encounters. Moreover, the vehicle does not only look like it is unfit to enter into confrontation with illegal trespassers, it simply is unable to perform this task. The machine has no weaponry, neither lethal nor non-lethal, but only a loudspeaker that can command the trespasser to leave the territory. On top of that, European law prohibits the robot to actually collide with the trespasser, making a real confrontation literally impossible. To this day, the machine cannot even perform its very limited tasks, as it was disassembled in 2012. Immediately after the European support stopped, each organisation took out the parts it created, thus leaving nothing of Talos except for a vague promise.

The ultimate outcome of the TALOS project should, however, not simply be measured against the actual production of an automated vehicle, but also against the production of a specific discourse, a singular vision that shapes our imagination of the future. Although TALOS seems incapable of creating a robotic system that can be deployed in border areas, the project's discourse paves the way for the future deployment of such a system. In a very subtle way TALOS intervenes in our imagination of the future, suggesting that the deployment of robotic systems is an inevitable and logical progression. It is perfectly possible that the consortium deliberately downplays the machine's aggressiveness, as this will ease us into the idea of using robots for border control. In other words, by giving the robot a friendly face the project makes it easier for us to imagine the deployment of robots in border areas. It is also in this respect that we should understand the reference to the Greek mythology. This reference generates a lineage between ancient Greece, commonly understood as one of the foundations of the European tradition, and the future deployment of robotic technologies for border securitisation. By using this reference, the project implicitly suggests that the usage of robotic power to secure borders is ingrained in Europe's DNA. TALOS' reference to Greek mythology should thus not be understood as a way to create a connection with a past event, but rather as a powerful means to employ the mythical figure to shape our vision on the future.

3. Talos, a Performance

The confrontation with Talos' double life was the starting point for the artistic research project that resulted in *Talos* (2016), a performance that reconciles an academic lecture, a sales pitch, and a story. When entering the venue, the spectators are confronted with the abstracted image of a border, projected on a screen that takes up the entire back wall. As will be only revealed later on in the performance, these animated images are based on drone footage of real border areas. The people in the original footage are replaced by dots and all other elements are substituted by their symbolic representation (for example, a real car is replaced by the symbol of a car). This abstract animation makes the videos resemble instructional videos or computer simulations rather than real-life situations. After a while, a man (Zaides) enters the stage and starts analyzing the image. His analysis is clearly scripted, as he reads the text from autocues that are positioned throughout the room. The description is precise and meticulous, and includes all the different forms, relations, and movements that are visible in the image. Despite this high level of precision, the analysis is marked by abstraction and detachment. Similar to the animation, the performer refrains from using concrete names for the elements, describing the people for example, who are depicted as dots, as 'moving entities'.

After analyzing five different border situations, the performer shifts his attention from the screen to the audience. This transition is reinforced by the background colour of the projection screen, which changes from grey to bright yellow. The analysis of borders now makes way for a presentation of a robotic vehicle: Talos. As a consummate salesman, the performer, who is still reading his text from the autocues, starts explaining the TALOS project, defining the vehicle's different features, the context in which it has to perform and the solutions that it can bring for potential users. At first, this explanation resembles the original European TALOS project, most of the time quoting documents that originate from the actual project. Gradually however, the text moves away from the original source material and explores more general developments in robotics.

This straying from the 'facts' culminates when the performance segues into the final part, dealing with the actual encounter between a trespasser and the machine. Where earlier parts were all based on documentary material, this part is almost entirely 'fabulated', based on the previously gathered/shared information. Once more accompanied by abstract animations of border situations, the performer imagines what the actual encounter between the robot and the trespasser might look like. Again, he refrains from concrete language. Moreover, his descriptions become even more abstract. Where in the first part the description was anchored in a specific situation, he now merely postulates general rules for an encounter to happen. Using a conditional 'if-then' proposition, the description meticulously maps out the different encounters that are possible in border areas and imagines how the vehicle could respond to this situation in a performant and effective way.

4. From Restoration to Creation: Two Times Re-enactment

Rather than aiming at reconstructing an original event, the performance in fact questions the reality of the 'original document'. Following performance theorist Carol Martin we could see the complexification of the document's status as a technique to draw the spectators' attention to the fact that 'reality is constructed', thus redirecting 'single perspective notions of truth toward the ambiguity of multiple viewpoints'.[6] Although we agree with Martin, it would, however, be a mistake to reduce the stakes of this performance to simply laying bare the fictional, or theatrical character of the document. Pointing out what is fictional or what is real is not relevant here. Although many documents originate from the TALOS project, a large number of documents were found in other places–interviews with experts, YouTube clips, mythology, and so on–and whole parts are made up. Moreover, the distinctions between the parts that are based on actual documents and the parts that are imagined is blurred, as all elements have the same status. The spectators do not know if this information is true, as it is clear that Zaides does not always follow the original project by mixing information that is distilled from the actual TALOS project with more general information about robotic developments, and with fictional information. Real or invented: what matters is the documents' creative potential.

As the Greek philosopher Cornelius Castoriadis pointed out, essential to creation is not 'discovery' but an active constitution of the 'new'. The 'real' and the 'invented' are not opposites, but actually two states of the imaginary. In other words, imagination comes before both fiction and reality and is essential in the shaping of both. Everything is first invented/imagined and then perhaps realized, constituted, within a context (can be society, art, or other) that forms a particular reality.[7] Both real and fictional documents can shape our understanding of the present and/or open up possible imaginations of the future.

Talos, thus understood as a re-appearing document, is used to various ends. Neither the European project nor the performance re-create an ancient myth. Both projects try to grasp how the former project could resonate in a contemporary situation. They both investigate how the past could help shape the imagination of present and future. This is abundantly clear in TALOS. The project does not simply attempt to re-construct the long-lost mythical automaton.

Instead, it creates a fictitious continuity between past, present, and future. This continuity serves a dual purpose. In the first instance it frames the emergence of the robotic vehicle as 'unavoidable'. Its implicit claim is that the idea of the deployment of robots for border protection is not new, but has always existed. TALOS will simply resume its role as a warden of Europe. In the second instance, the continuity eliminates the many political and ethical questions that are conjured up by the deployment of robots for border protection. By associating it with a divine figure, TALOS gives the robotic vehicle an aura of necessity and objectivity. This objectivity is not granted by a divine force, but by an objective algorithm instead. Were in ancient times the actions of the robot were justified by the fact that they originated from a divine presence, the actions of the European vehicle for border control seem just, because they are the outcome of a transparent algorithmic procedure. Here, the project blends the ancient belief in the infallibility of divinity with the contemporary belief that, with the help of big data and algorithms to process this data, we can solve any problem. God has been replaced by the algorithm, but the underlying logic stays the same: TALOS does what it needs to do, will never make mistakes and will always be equitable. We should not doubt that Talos be instantiated in the future, as its emergence is inevitable—embedded in Europe's DNA—and its actions are objective: following a procedural logic that is quasi-divine.

By referring to the past in order to colonize the future, TALOS frames this future simply as the actualization of the past. This brought up the following question: how can an artistic project relate to this operational logic? In the first phase of the project, we discovered that strategies of re-enactment—building a land-drone—lose their potential as they would only point to the actual European project, laying bare its many flaws and problems but neglecting the implicit thread that the project weaves from past to future. We thus searched for a way to intervene in, or expose the 'territorialization' of the future that takes place in and through the European project. In order to do this. we decided to shift from the strategy of reconstruction towards pre-enactment, or from staging documents towards speculation.

This strategy also entails a re-conceptualization, or reframing of re-enactment. Often re-enactment is understood as an attempt to make something re-appear. It is conceived as an attempt to gain access to a past that has passed, by bringing the past back into the present. As Hal Foster mentions, re-enactment here functions as an articulation of the 'archival impulse'.[8] In turn, this impulse is the result of a 'failure in cultural memory', an attempt 'to probe a misplaced past'.[9] As such, re-enactment is always reactive. It starts from the historical consciousness, the awareness that time is progressive and creates a gap between past and present, and tries to find a way to deal with this gap.[10] However, this is not the case in the instantiation of the mythical figure described above. TALOS does not aim at re-creating the past. The project instead looks to the past for possible elements that would resonate with the future.

In his article 'The Body as Archive: Will to Re-Enact and the Afterlives of Dances' performance scholar André Lepecki tries to understand re-enactment as something that is not simply re-active, but also creative and active. For this description, Lepecki refers to Walter Benjamin's notion of 'afterlife'. According to Benjamin, the task of the translator is not to strive for 'likeness with the original', but to look for ways to transform the original so that it resonates with the contemporary context.[11] Similarly, re-enactment should not try to 'fix a work in its singular (originating) possibilization but to release a work's many *(in)compossibilities* ([im]possibilities of composing), which the originating instantiations kept in reserve, virtually'.[12] As such, a re-enactment is always also a *pre*-enactment. It pre-forms or pre-figures something that was already (potentially) present in the past and that can be actualized in the present in order to condition possible futures.

5. From Documentation to Speculation: Pre-enacting Talos

In economy the term 'speculation' refers to the investment in stocks, property, etc., in the hope of quick gains but with a huge risk of loss. In contemporary design, speculation might be about taking a risk with the unknown in a much more playful way that could potentially even undermine the notions of progress, profit, or loss. Speculative design is proposed as a tool to understand the present and to create space for discussion about where we would want to go from here collectively. It is important to realize that speculation is actually a way of engaging with the present; a way of 'staying with the trouble' as Donna Haraway advocates so strongly. 'Staying with the trouble', she writes, 'does not require such a relationship to times called the future. It requires learning to be truly present'.[13] One of her core methods of engaging with the present is 'speculative fabulation', which refers to everyday storytelling and the way in which people tell each other stories, or fables: 'wild facts'. Fabulation is the making of fables and a form of 'other world makings'. Just like pre-enactment and speculative design are forms of training, of redefining our relationship to reality, fabulation is also such a practice that should be taken seriously next to what we assume as 'truth' (science fact). Fabulation is part of the same figure through which we (can) try to understand the world we live in. Speculation is of big influence on our world today, used by thinkers and innovators in economy, technology, anthropology, ecology, and philosophy (accelerationism, speculative realism), literature (science fiction, speculative fiction, afro-futurism), art and not seldomly several of those combined–as a strategy to open up a space to discuss/imagine/think about the future.

During our residence in Vienna, political philosopher Oliver Marchart was the first to introduce the notion of pre-enactment. It is a notion we have come to understand as a specific way of speculating. According to Marchart, we can define pre-enactment as an 'artistic anticipation of a political event to come'.[14] This anticipation, however, should not be understood as an analytical tool through which we 'critically extrapolate from contemporary developments an image of our social and political future', but as a 'pre-formance', an act through which we pre-figure, or pre-form the future.[15] Rather than making a prognosis about the future, the pre-enactment actively shapes it. To understand this process of 'pre-forming', philosopher and artist Patricia Reed provides insight. In her text 'Reorientate, Eccentricate, Speculate, Fictionalize, Geometricize, Commonize, Abstractify: Seven Prescriptions for Accelerationism' (2014) she distinguishes between prognostics and speculation. According to Reed, prognostics equate the future with anticipation. Here, the future simply is the actualization of certain threads that are already present in past and present. As such, the future remains 'in the temporality of what is (or what was)'. Speculation however, is an attempt to (pre)shape the unknown future: 'directing existing energies in (as yet) inexistent directions'.[16] Reed connects this 'speculative possibility' with the notions of fiction and fabulation. Rather than simply predicting the future, speculation actively fabulates the future by mapping 'vectors of the future upon the present'.[17]

Returning to our Taloses with these insights, both the European TALOS project and *Talos* (the performance) could be viewed as the 'strategy' of pre-enactment, but to very different ends. The European project actively promotes ideas on surveillance at the continent's borders through the use of technological devices, and intends to implement a (feeling of) need for those developments. Their demonstrator is not a question up for debate, but an idea that 'we can get used to', and mostly, a potential product for the European surveillance market. It seems a way of 'mapping vectors of the future upon the present'[18] that is quite violent as it tries to enforce a certain ideology/politics. This may be the reason for the project's pre-formative, speculative character being hidden. The project suggests a certain future but does not make this future explicit. Moreover, it masks its goals by representing its vision of the future as a simple continuation of present and past. As such, TALOS functions as a smooth operator, selling its speculation as mere prognostics. Seeing the TALOS Wall-E lookalike as speculative design 'in disguise' makes it more political and more detrimental then it seemed at first. In this light, without even existing anymore or yet, the *idea* of the TALOS *to be* would already be an actual event (a pre-enactment).

For this reason, we accepted the task to make the speculative character of the European project explicit, and as such open up the future that TALOS pre-forms and enable a debate about that future. One aspect specifically compelled our attention upon examining the European TALOS project. This was the absence of the actual encounter between the machine and the trespasser, in both the visual and textual documents that were available on the project.[19] One would expect that TALOS–like his Greek predecessors–would be focused on his main target: the trespasser. The film *Jason and the Argonauts* (1963) by Don Chaffey for example emphasizes how the bronze giant defends his lady Europa, as he basically lifts the intruders' ship from the sea and shakes it with ease until all passengers are flung towards their deaths. A scene reminiscent of immigrant dramas happening on many international waters today where the 'violent giant' has many appearances. None of the documents that were produced by the European consortium however discuss the actual encounter with 'illegal bodies'.

In the performance *Talos*, Zaides and his team consequently tried to think through the operational logic of the automated vehicle. By adopting strategies of generalization that transform concrete situations into abstract models and political/ethical processes of decision-making into mechanic operations, the performance crystallized the encounter between the human and the machine that would take place at the border. In other words, *Talos* explicitly pre-formed what the European TALOS project merely suggested.

This speculative mapping creates a double-edged feeling. In the first instance, the viewer comes to understand the violence that is contained in the logarithmic reduction of human interactions to a series of if-then-propositions. This cruelty becomes abundantly clear towards the very end of the performance, when the animated images transform into the real drone footage. Suddenly the dots, or moving entities, become individual human beings. At the same time, however, the spectators are confronted with the futility, or vanity of this project. It becomes clear that the procedural logic of the vehicle will never be able to respond to the concrete situation in an adequate way, as it is impossible to reduce the endlessly complex real-life situations with actual people to a fixed set of variables and constants. As such, *Talos* manages to lay bare the atrocities which TALOS sweeps under the rug, but also shows how the project is in itself based on a fiction: the fiction that technical developments and procedural logics are natural or necessary and that they will solve all our problems.

6. Pre-forming Futures

What should we use speculation for? In the light of technological developments, the act of speculation touches upon one of the biggest questions we are faced with: how do we want to develop as humankind? Or: what kind of people do we want to be (within this world)? 'To speculate', Reed writes, 'is to articulate and enable the contingencies of the given, armed only with the certainty that what is, is always incomplete; to speculate is to play with the demonstration of this innately porous, nontotalisable set of givens'.[20] This quotation beautifully describes what we attempted with our approach in *Talos*. Moreover, Reed's notion underlines speculation as an act of engagement. An engagement with the present perhaps, a present (both real and invented) world in which we wonder; 'what future do we want to see performed?' This question seems to be burning in more and more people. Not because we want to know what lies ahead, but on the contrary, because we want the future back as a *multitude of inexistent directions.* Some of us have the feeling that the future is being hijacked, that particular versions of the future are being produced by Silicon Valley and other high-tech developers into consumable Musk-ian futurisms. Haraway warns against this kind of naïve 'techno-fixes': the idea that in the face of all global crises–of immigration, ecology, or other–'technology will come to the rescue of us all'. The European consortium developed the TALOS border surveillance drone exactly as such a product. Through pre-enacting the inherent promise, their idea carried a *dataist* ideology of sorts: such a future that 'will save us [from immigrants]'. If we do not want to see our future performed for us, the question becomes: what future do we ourselves wish to perform, pre-form, pre-enact?

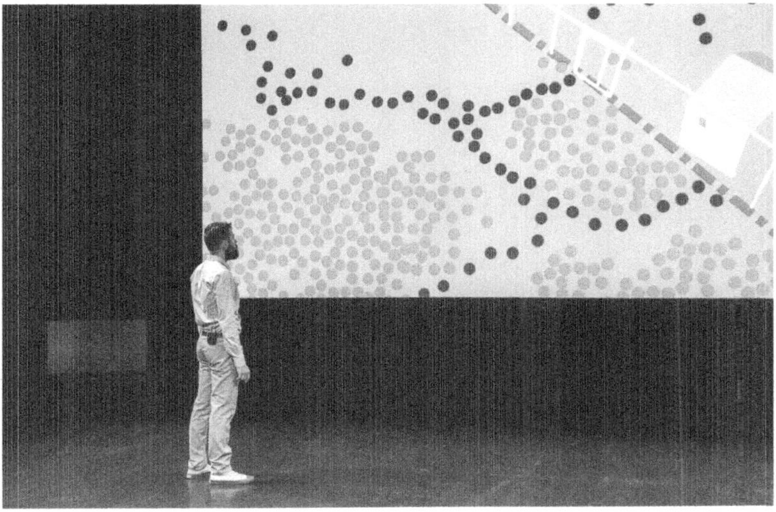

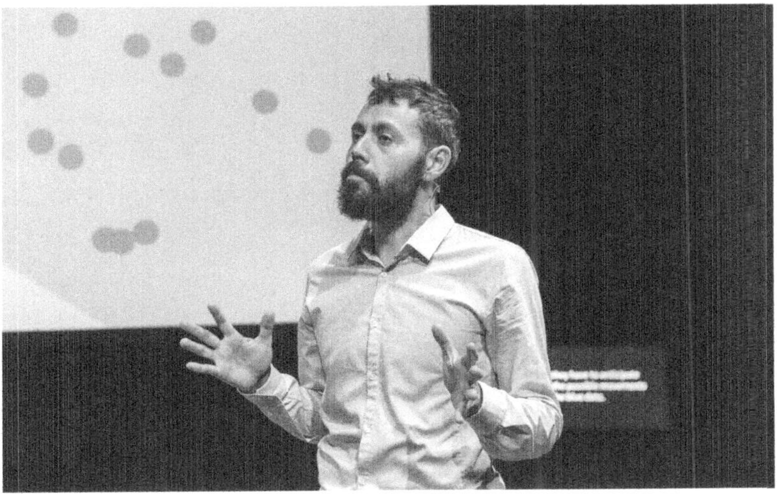

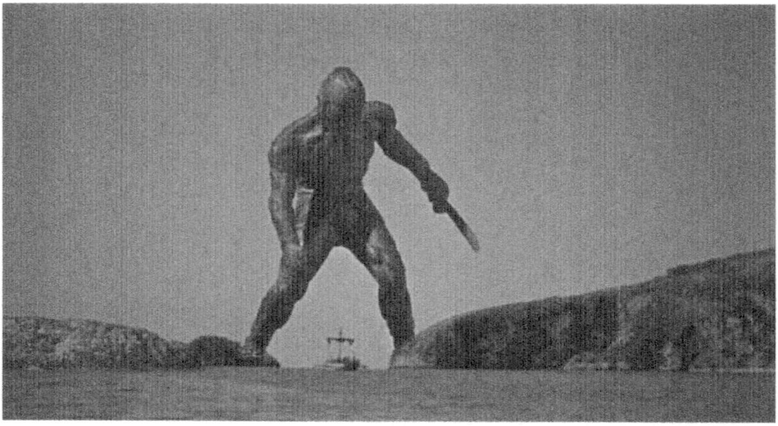

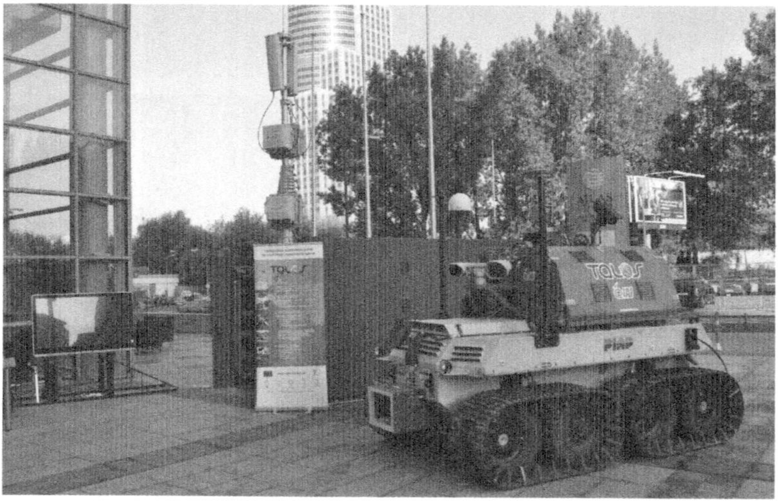
TALOS
PIAP

Images

- *Talos*, a performance by Arkadi Zaides, festival Tanz im August, HAU Hebbel, Berlin, August 2017. Photographer: Dajana Lothert
- Close up of choreographer Arkadi Zaides, festival Tanz im August, HAU Hebbel, Berlin, August 2017. Photographer: Dajana Lothert
- Still from the film *Jason and the Argonauts* by Don Chaffey, 1963
- *Talos*, a performance by Arkadi Zaides, festival Tanz im August, HAU Hebbel, Berlin, August 2017. Photographer: Dajana Lothert

Notes

1 The performance *Talos* premiered in Hebbel am Ufer (Berlin) on 30 August 2017. It was a collaboration between Arkadi Zaides, who initiated the project and had the artistic lead, and Claire Buisson, Nienke Scholts, Jonas Rutgeerts, Youness Anzane, Effi & Amir (Effi Weiss & Amir Borenstein), Gabriel Braga, Culture Crew, Amit Epstein, and Dyane Neiman. The research also involved experts from different fields, who were invited to give their take on the project and whose input in turn enriched the project.

2 The main objective of TALOS was to develop and field-test a semi-autonomous robotic system for protecting European land borders. The project budget amounts to 20 million euros, 13 million of which has been funded by the EU 7th Framework Programme in Security priority. TALOS was developed by experts working for 14 institutions from 8 EU member states as well as two associated countries. The partners were: Przemysłowy Instytut Automatyki i Pomiarów, Poland; ASELSAN Elektronik Sanayi ve Ticaret A.S, Turkey; European Business Innovation & Research Center S.A, Romania; Hellenic Aerospace Industry S.A., Greece; Israel Aerospace Industries, Israel; ITTI Sp. z o.o., Poland; Office National d'Etudes et de Recherches, France; Smartdust Solutions, Estonia; SONACA S.A., Belgium; STM Savunma Teknolojileri Mühendislik ve Ticaret A.S., Turkey; Telekomunikacja Polska S.A., Poland; TTI Norte S.L., Spain; VTT Technical Research Centre of Finland; Politechnika Warszawska, Poland.

3 The figure of Talos does appear in other contexts before Apollonius Rhodius' *The Argonautica.* There even are detailed images of the episode dated to around 400 BC. His multitude of appearances caused some confusion about the origin and the characteristics of his person. He appears in different shapes throughout Greek mythology: as the brazen bull-shaped creation given by Hephaestus/ Vulcan to Minos to protect Crete, as a talented smith who rivalled Hephaestus and invented the saw, the

potter's wheel and even the compass, or as a civil servant of Crete who went through the villages in order to uphold the law, and carried with him the laws written in tables of brass (Plato). However, it is safe to say that the most detailed and most clear description of the figure can be found in Rhodius' epic poem. (See: Brian Sparkes, *The Red and The Black: Studies in Greek pottery* [New York: Routledge, 1996], p. 124).

4 The partners of the consortium worked together to build two vehicles that would be deployed along the borders of the European Union. First, there is the Unmanned Ground Patroller. This robotic ground vehicle is equipped with long-range sensors and a hybrid engine, and is able to operate in a so-called 'stealth' mode. Its task is to detect intruders. Second, there is the Unmanned Ground Interceptor. This is a robotic ground vehicle too, but one that is equipped with precise optical sensors and loudspeakers and is deployed to track already detected intruders and to deliver verbal messages. The two vehicles are supplied with an immobile sensor tower that provides 'permanent observation of important geographical points, like fords or forest roads', an unmanned air unit, a robotic aircraft equipped with long-range sensors for the detection of intruders, and an unmanned units command centre, which is a container filled with consoles for operators and commanders of the robotic units.

5 MichalTanas et al., 'The TALOS Project: EU wide robotic border guard system', in *16th International Conference on Methods & Models in Automation & Robotics* (proceedings), Mi dzyzdroje 2011, p. 336.

6 Carol Martin, 'History and Politics: The Theatre of the Real', in *Not Just a Mirror: Looking for the Political Theatre Today*, ed. Florian Malzacher (Berlin: Alexander Verlag, 2015), p. 37.

7 CorneliusCastoriadis, *The Imaginary Institution of Society* (London: Polity Press, 1975) p. 133.

8 Hal Foster, 'An Archival Impulse', *October* 110 (2004), p. 3.

9 Ibid., p. 21.

10 This 'dealing with' can be conceived in different ways. One the one hand one can search for ways to revive the authentic past. On the other hand, this bringing back of the past into the present can also be conceptualized in a reflexive way. Here, the focus is on the fact that the past can never become present, and the absence of the past in the present.

11 Walter Benjamin, *Gesammelte Schriften* (Frankfurt am Main: Suhrkamp, 1974), p. 256.

12 André Lepecki, 'The Body as Archive: Will to Re-enact and the Afterlives of Dances', *Dance Research Journal* 42, no. 2 (2010), p. 31.

13 Donna Haraway, *Staying with the Trouble: Making Kin in the Chthulucene* (Durham, NC: Duke University Press, 2016), p. 1.

14 Oliver Marchart, 'Public Movement: The Art of Pre-enactment', in *Not Just a Mirror: Looking for the Political Theatre Today*, ed. Florian Malzacher (Berlin: Alexander Verlag, 2015), p. 149.

15 Ibid., p. 146.

16 Patricia Reed, 'Reorientate, Eccentricate, Speculate, Fictionalize, Geometricize, Commonize, Abstractify: Seven Prescriptions for Accelerationism', in *#ACCELERATE: The Accelerationist Reader*, eds. Robin Mackay and Armen Avanessian (Falmouth: Urbanomic and Merve Verlag, 2014), p. 524.

17 Ibid., p. 529.

18 As Marchart stated during one of the meetings: 'In the TALOS project nothing is *re*-enacted, not even a Greek myth. What we witness is a moment of *pre-enactment*–a moment of anticipation'.

19 This avoidance becomes abundantly clear in the promotional video. Rather than explaining the qualities of the vehicle, the interviewees mainly focus on the fact that the collaboration between the international partners was enriching. On the actual performance of the vehicle, they refer to the difficulties in designing a robot that is able to both drive autonomously and to manoeuvre through rough terrain. Not a single word is mentioned about the actual task of the machine: interacting with trespassers and impeding their movement.

20 Reed, 'Reorientate, Eccentricate, Speculate...', p. 527.

Sensuous Science
On the Threshold between Fact and Fiction—An Afterword

Pascal Gielen

> The only realist option is to do what appears impossible within this system. This is how the impossible becomes possible.
> Slavoj Žižek, 2013

Aesthetic Horizon

If, as Slavoy Žižek suggests, the duty of philosophy today is to 'think the impossible', then it is perhaps the societal duty of the activist to demand the impossible and the moral obligation of the artist to make that same impossibility audible, visible, and tangible. If the sciences are concerned with the possibility of a new reality, then art is concerned with realizing the impossible. Yet rarely since the dawn of modernity have artists been given their own laboratory to do so, regardless of whether they are active at art academies or in their own studios, or producing a play or a novel. The safely demarcated space of fiction is what allows the artist to tinker with reality. This doesn't mean messing around aimlessly–although that's certainly part of it. As every artist well knows, they have, since the dawn of modernity, been permitted one thing and one thing only: to produce something new. Even in the wake of post-modernity, this progressive desire still dominates the artistic brain.

Just like thinkers are only worthy of the title 'philosopher' when they come up with a new idea, artists are only deemed worthy as such when they have developed a new *sign*. However immaterial an artistic act may be, it is always expected to add something to that great cauldron of symbols we call 'culture'. While the latter is perpetuated through the conservation of rituals, habits, traditions, values, and norms, the artists know that it is up to them to keep dismantling it. Still, however much the historical avant-garde would have you believe it, even the most powerful art does not shatter any traditions. At most it adds a fine layer, while the underlying layer deteriorates and is sometimes forgotten. Indeed, artists add things and rarely dismantle anything–let alone permanently destroy them–except for when it comes to their own work. Which makes every artist a vitalist. However sombre the future might look, the artist will always have the fiery impulse to add something. Creation rests, after all, on the intense drive to live, the drive to live and create life ferociously, intensely, and indeed dangerously.

In this respect, artists do not differ greatly from scientists. To discover new knowledge the driven scientist will similarly pull out all the stops. Whether they are observing the movements of micro-organisms or those of a crowd of people, researchers hope to report enriching insights. Even scientific scepticism and critical theory, in all their endless doubt, pessimism, and negativity, betray a degree of vitalism. The scientist nurses the quiet hope that their critical spirit will at least contribute something of value to the world, if not an abundance. This is perhaps the real difference between art and science: while scientists test new possibilities against reality, artists are primarily interested in what reality does not allow. The former train their efforts on arriving at a new reality, the latter on bringing out that which escapes reality. At the very least, scientists must convince their peers, or a certain community, of a new reality, relying on approved instruments to verify their claims: logical proof, a repeatable method or an accurate measuring instrument. Artists, on the other hand, must draw on experience. In their case, the primacy of persuasiveness beats out the burden of proof. While science must prove itself through repeatability and reason, artists convince by presenting a singular experience that appeals to aesthesis–sensual perception.

So much for the now-trite distinction between science and art or, for that matter, fact and fiction. Much more interesting indeed is the space in between. Or, to invoke Žižek again, the borderland between the possible and the impossible. With the notion of the 'aesthetic horizon', Alexander Gottlieb Baumgarten (1750–58) understood this border not as a fine line but as an extensible area where logic and aesthetics touch and sometimes become inextricably combined. Here, in Leonardo da Vinci's element, cognitive and sensitive horizons overlap, with the burden of proof and the primacy of persuasiveness encroaching on each other's waters. Here, there is no longer any hard border to be drawn between fact and fiction; the separation is rather more gradual. Things are simply more fact or more fiction, ambiguously interstitial.

The Base

In an era when populism, alternative facts and fake news reign, it is understandable that the academic world would champion the idea that there is in fact a clear line between fact and fiction. The fear of being swept up or indeed abused by populist rhetoric makes Baumgarten's grey area of ambiguous knowledge less popular, suspect even. The age-old liaison between fact and fiction is thus more readily rejected. This often results in stiff academicism, where the method prevails over common sense. Or where a scientifically sound methodology determines what counts as relevant knowledge, and not vice versa. In striving for self-preservation, the scientific establishment thus obscures the crucial role fiction serves in it. We might do well to take seriously Baumgarten's idea that the aesthetic lies *infra horizontem*, under the cognitive horizon. That our cognitive capacity rests on a highly sensitive foundation. In this way, imagination is to science as labour relations were to society for Karl Marx. It is the base, not the superstructure. Is that not after all the meaning of 'scientific intuition'? Scientific facts are built on fictions, on the imaginary, on our capacity to picture something in our minds. To put it another way, the sturdy house of self-assured science was built on a much less self-assured substratum of intuitions, imaginings and speculations. There are no hypotheses without imagination, no laboratory experiments without fictive presuppositions about reality. In short, fiction precedes fact. Scientists are constantly testing their imaginary projections against reality. Stringent methods and measuring instruments are used to verify or falsify these projections in order to arrive at scientific fact or proof. It remains the case, however, that scientific fact is to a large extent determined by the nature of the presuppositions against which it is tested. The discovery of scientific facts indeed depends on the imagination of the researchers or, for that matter, the aesthetic horizon on which they approach their research subject. Similarly, social facts are largely determined based on the questions the sociologist does or does not ask about the social reality. In other words, these facts depend heavily on the sociologists' imaginative capacity and what they deem to be either possible or impossible. This is also true outside of the humanities. Was the particle collider at CERN not built to test unproven theories against reality? Here, too, the aesthetic horizon of a number of computer scientists determined what we would later call 'natural law'. There is surely nothing more artistic than an unproven theory: the design of something that does not yet exist and perhaps never will. This is thinking on the border of the impossible and the possible, reasoning within Baumgarten's aesthetic horizon.

Savage Thought

Not only do aesthetics form the foundation on which the house of scientific truth is built, but our aesthetic capacity offers the building blocks for a methodology that could lead us to a different kind of knowledge. A whole other *species* of knowledge, indeed one that stands alone alongside other kinds of (scientific) knowledge. As such it would encompass a form and capacity of knowing that would not only complement but also reinforce pre-accumulated knowledge. Whereas dancers, for example, sense their bodies and after much training know what they are capable of, biologists, via a completely different methodological path, may arrive at the same knowledge. Likewise, sculptors understand the stone they hew differently from geologists, who reduce the stone to its smallest particles for observation. While artists become familiar with their material through aesthesis, scientists use their gaze primarily to detachedly understand the same thing. While the former try to grasp their world from within, the latter do so from the outside. The first touches, smells, listens, feels and resonates with the subject, while the latter looks, fixates and categorizes. Aesthetics are in this way a visceral science. The artist amasses subjective, the scientist objective knowledge.

As is widely known, following the Enlightenment, detached observation, rationality and abstraction gained the upper hand in scientific practices, while knowledge gained through empathy, touching, and feeling was relegated to the realm of fiction. Yet both approaches yield complementary knowledge. While the first gave us GPS, with which we can confidently reach our destination via binary codes and coordinates, the second draws our attention to the smells, colours, and undulations of the landscape we are travelling through. It is perhaps no coincidence that it was a self-made anthropologist who understood the value of art in this way. Claude Lévi-Strauss (1966) considered contemporary artistic expression a modern form of 'savage thought', a type of knowledge that he believed to be level pegging with science. Indeed, anthropology pays a great deal of attention to the indigenous customs of a local culture within its natural environment. This sensitivity for the subjective, the 'experienced' use of the world and the things in it, reveals much more about the *value* of culture and nature than a detached survey, for example. For this reason, it would perhaps be wise for the current scientific establishment to reconsider the value of aesthetics as providing a tangible knowledge of the world. Those who familiarize themselves with culture and nature through direct use recognize its import: the farmer who cultivates the land understands only too well when it has fallen fallow, just as a home owner senses the house's creaking and groaning as it wears with age. In the same way, dancers are skilled in sensing the space through which they move, as well as the possibilities and boundaries of objects and people with whom they connect during a performance. In short, aesthetic knowing sharpens our sense of finitude and permanency. What the GPS does not reveal is how the landscape erodes, how its scents and colours change as and, in part, *because* we are passing through it. The GPS simply tells us the best or fastest route from point A to point B. This most intelligent device doesn't teach us how to value, use, and consume the road and the landscape. This we only grasp when we look up from the screen and let the world in through all of our senses.

It is not enough to think the impossible and to (permit) experience. Most crucially, today's artists must do this in concert with their sense of finitude. It is precisely this aesthetic capacity, this internal understanding of the world, that science still lacks. Only through aesthesis can we connect with our environment. As such, it is the role of art to immerse us all in that world–scientists included.

Literature

— Baumgarten, Alexander G. *Ästhetik* (1750-58). Hamburg: Meiner Felix Verlag, 2009
— Lévi-Strauss, Claude. *The Savage Mind*. London: Weidenfeld and Nicholson, 1966
— Žižek, Slavoj. *Demanding the Impossible*. Cambridge, MA: Polity Press 2013

About the Authors

Pascal Gielen is professor of sociology of culture and politics at the Antwerp Research Institute for the Arts (Belgium) where he leads the Culture Commons Quest Office (CCQO). Gielen is editor of the international book series Antennae–Arts in Society (Valiz). In 2016 he became laureate of the Odysseus grant for excellent international scientific research of the Fund for Scientific Research Flanders in Belgium. Gielen has published many books, some of which have been translated into Chinese, English, Polish, Portuguese, Russian, Spanish, Turkish and Ukrainian. His research focuses on creative labour, the common, urban and cultural politics. Gielen works and lives in Antwerp, Belgium. www.ccqo.eu, www.uantwerpen.be/en/research-groups/aria/

Andrea Gorki studied painting at Naples Academy of Fine Arts and Offenbach University of Art and Design. She was the managing director of the art space Rückseite in Berlin and is a co-founder and editor of the magazine *Feld*. She is currently a Master's student in economics at the Freie Universität Berlin.

Charlotte Lybeer studied photography at the Royal Academy of Fine Arts Ghent and post-graduated at the Higher Institute for Fine Arts (HISK) in Antwerp. In 2016 she received her PhD in visual arts (Lifestyle Supermarket) at the Royal Academy of Fine Arts Antwerp, where she's teaching photography. Lybeer's photography projects were widely exhibited nationally as well as abroad (including the Flemish Institute Osaka JP, the Kunsthal, Rotterdam, Liefhertje en De Grote Witte Reus, The Hague, Three Shadows Photography Art Center, Beijing, Flanders House, New York and published in leading journals and magazines (*Camera Austria*, *NRC Handelsblad*, *Americansuburbx*, *GUP Magazine*, *Metropolis M*, *Capricious Magazine*). Her work is also documented extensively through her website charlottelybeer.be. In 2016 she made two books: *Epidermis II* (Art Paper Editions) and *Encyclopedia, Incomplete from A to Z* (self-published), in which she confronts her own work with photography from the Dutch National Archive's Spaarnestad Photo collection. In 2019, The Royal Academy of Fine Arts Antwerp published Lybeer's series *Linus' Blanket*.

Sigrid Merx is an assistant professor Theatre Studies at Utrecht University, where she teaches in the BA program Media and Culture and in the MA programmes Contemporary Theatre, Dance and Dramaturgy and Arts and Society. She is one of the core members of the [urban interfaces] research group and one of the initiators of Platform-Scenography, a platform invested in deepening the understanding of scenographic working and thinking. She occasionally works as a dramaturge and curator. Her current research focuses on critical performative interventions in public space that reflect on issues of the urban, publicness, and civic engagement and on creative methods of investigating, mapping, and intervening in public spaces.

Patrícia Portela is a writer and performance maker who lives in both Belgium and Portugal. She studied set and costume design in Lisbon, dramaturgy of space in Utrecht and Antwerp, film in Ebeltoft, Denmark, and Philosophy in Leuven, Belgium. Since 2003 she has worked on her own performances and installations in international collaborations with other artists. She has achieved national and international recognition for her unusual work and is considered one of the most daring artists and innovative writers of her generation. In 1994 she won the Revelation Prize for her creative work in performance and cinema, the Prize Teatro na Década for *T5* in 1999, the Gulbenkian Foundation Prize Madalena de Azeredo Perdigão for the performance *Flatland I* in 2004, and was one of the five finalists of the Sonae Media Art Prize 2015 with her installation *Parasomnia*, among other prizes. She has been invited to participate in the prestigious International Writing Program (IWP) at the University of Iowa in 2013 and to be the first Outreach Fellow, and she was the first literary resident in Berlin in 2016, sponsored by the Portuguese Embassy in Germany/Instituto Camões. She regularly lectures dramaturgy and space at Universities and cultural centres in Portugal (such as University of Minho or University of Lisbon) and elsewhere (University of Antwerp, or escola de escrita in Curitiba). She is the author of several novels, short stories and performances, and has been a chronicle writer for the prestigious *Jornal de Letras* since 2017, as well as for the Portuguese National Radio Antena 1.

Jonas Rutgeerts is a dramaturge and performance maker based in Belgium. He obtained his PhD in Philosophy from the Institute of Philosophy (KU Leuven) and is currently affiliated with the Centre for Cultural Studies (KU Leuven). As a dramaturge and researcher, he collaborated with Needcompany, Ivana Müller, David Weber-Krebs, Clément Layes and Arkadi Zaides, among others. He is the author of *Re-act: Over re-enactment in de hedendaagse dans* (Tectum Verlag, 2015).

Nienke Scholts is a freelance dramaturge and programme maker. She works/ed with several performance artists, and Veem House for Performance (2013–2019), in collaboration with whom she developed the multi-voiced publication series Words for the Future (2017–2018). She is a fellow of THIRD at DASresearch (AHK), and programme coordinator of ARIAS Amsterdam platform for discipline-transgressing research practices. Other recent writings include 'Dramaturges That Do Not Work For A Work', in *The Practice of Dramaturgy* (Valiz, 2016) and 'Zorg, ergens aan gaan staan' in *nY magazine* #37. She is also co-founder and editor of Platform-Scenography (P-S), and an inspired bee-keeper apprentice.

Belgian-Polish **Katharina Smets** moulds documentary materials into performances, sound guides, and radio productions. Fascinated by memories and archives, her collaborations with other artists and musicians invariably start from a shared need to give voice to vulnerable stories. Currently working on a PhD in the arts, Katharina teaches audio storytelling at the Royal Conservatoire in Antwerp. Katharina curates the audio story festival Oorzaken in Amsterdam and she is a proud co-founder of MIRP, the Meeting of Independent Radio Producers.

Elly Van Eeghem works as an artist on the meaning, design, and use of the urbanized landscape. Her work consists of videos, photography, writing, actions, and installations in public space. She makes individual works as well as collective projects in collaboration with local residents, school children, or fellow artists. Her touring work, *(Dis)placed Interventions*, earned her a PhD in the Arts at KASK School of Arts Ghent, where she is currently still teaching.

Peter Van Goethem is a director, an author and a painter. His doctoral research in the arts, *De filmregisseur als* *archivaris* (The movie director as an archivist) at the Free University of Brussels and the Royal Institute for Theatre, Cinema and Sound (RITCS), explored the relationship between arts/aesthetics and urbanity.

Taking as his starting point an inventory of non-fiction film fragments featuring the (Brussels) cityscape, he built a portfolio including the found footage film *Night Has Come* (2018) (using existing archival material from the inventory), the novel *Restitutie* (Restitution) (2018) and a series of painted portraits called *Tipping Point* (2018).

Stefan Vanthuyne is a writer, researcher, and photographer. He regularly writes about photography and photobooks for the Belgian newspaper *De Standaard*. His articles have also been published in *Knack Focus*, *Oogst*, *EXTRA (FOMU)*, *1000 Words* Aperture's *The PhotoBook Review*, and other publications. As a researcher he is affiliated with the Royal Academy of Fine Arts Antwerp, where his main topic is the contemporary Belgian photobook. In 2017 he started the Belgian Platform for Photobooks. He is a member of the photography research group Thinking Tools, also at the Royal Academy of Fine Arts Antwerp, and of the editorial board of *FORUM*+, the peer-reviewed journal in research and arts.

Ludovik Vermeersch is a visual artist, writer, and curator. He has written for numerous art journals and worked on several research projects, most recently at the University of Antwerp and St. Lucas School of Arts Antwerp. In 2015, he published the book *Personally, I'm Most Interested in the Shapes and Colours* (MER. Paper Kunsthalle), which accompanied his eponymous lecture performance. Since 2012, he has been a curator at Kunstraum Ossastraße Berlin.

Nele Wynants is a postdoctoral researcher in the fields of art and theatre at the Free University of Brussels-ULB and the University of Antwerp. Her work on the interplay of performance, media history and science has appeared in many journals and books. She is editor-in-chief of *FORUM*+ for research and arts (www.forum-online.be) and her edited volume *Media Archaeology and Intermedial Performance: Deep Time of the Theatre* recently appeared with Palgrave Macmillan.

Index

Colophon

Colophon

When Fact Is Fiction
Documentary Art in the Post-Truth Era

Editor
Nele Wynants

Contributors
Pascal Gielen
Andrea Gorki
Charlotte Lybeer
Sigrid Merx
Patrícia Portela
Jonas Rutgeerts
Nienke Scholts
Katharina Smets
Elly Van Eeghem
Peter Van Goethem
Stefan Vanthuyne
Ludovik Vermeersch
Nele Wynants

Antennae-Arts *in* Society Series N° 28
by Valiz, Amsterdam

Copy Editing
Leo Reijnen, Els Brinkman

Proofreading
Els Brinkman

Index
Elke Stevens

Design
Metahaven

Paper Inside
Munken Print 100 gr 1.5

Paper Cover
Bioset 240 gr

Printing and Binding
Bariet Ten Brink, Meppel
POD: Scanlaser, Zaandam

Publisher
Valiz, Amsterdam, 2020
Second print, POD, 2024
www.valiz.nl

ISBN 978-94-92095-71-8
This publication was made possible through the generous support of:

Artesis Plantijn University College, Antwerp

Antwerp Research Institute for the Arts (ARIA), Antwerp

The chapters 'Imaginations of Reality' by Nele Wynants, 'The Private Collection of Acácio Nobre' by Patrícia Portela, 'The Fragile I' by Katharina Smets, 'Between Realities #Athens' by Sigrid Merx, '(Dis) placed interventions' by Elly Van Eeghem and 'TALOS/Talos' by Jonas Rutgeerts and Nienke Scholts have been published in Dutch in the journal *FORUM*⁺ for research and arts (www.forum-online.be).

Antennae-Arts in Society
Antennae-Arts in Society is a peer-reviewed book series that validates artistic, critical, speculative and essayistic writing as a full academic publishing method. Contributions to the series look upon the arts as 'antennae', feelers for the cultural interpretation and articulation of topical political, economic, social, technological or environmental issues.

The books in this series bring together audiences of diverse backgrounds: artists and other creative makers, academics and researchers from various disciplines, critics, writers, journalists, politicians, curators, and institutional parties, who wish to broaden their view in different political, social and other contexts.

Proposals for book concepts in all artistic and scientific disciplines that take culture as the base of interpretation for the social fabric of our contemporary lives are welcomed and will be considered for publication by the academic board.

Distribution:
USA/Canada/Latin America: D.A.P., www.artbook.com
GB/IE: Anagram Books, www.anagrambooks.com
NL/BE/LU: Centraal Boekhuis, www.cb.nl
Europe/Asia: Idea Books, www.ideabooks.nl
Australia: Perimeter Books, www.perimeterdistribution.com

ISBN 978-94-92095-71-8

Printed and bound in the Netherlands

Antennae

Antennae Series

Antennae N° 1
The Fall of the Studio
Artists at Work
edited by Wouter Davidts & Kim Paice
Amsterdam: Valiz, 2009
(2nd ed.: 2010),
ISBN 978-90-78088-29-5

Antennae N° 2
Take Place
Photography and Place from Multiple Perspectives
edited by Helen Westgeest
Amsterdam: Valiz, 2009,
ISBN 978-90-78088-35-6

Antennae N° 3
The Murmuring of the Artistic Multitude
Global Art, Memory and Post-Fordism
Pascal Gielen (author)
Arts *in* Society
Amsterdam: Valiz, 2009
(2nd ed.: 2011),
ISBN 978-90-78088-34-9

Antennae N° 4
Locating the Producers
Durational Approaches to Public Art
edited by Paul O'Neill & Claire Doherty
Amsterdam: Valiz, 2011, ISBN 978-90-78088-51-6

Antennae N° 5
Community Art
The Politics of Trespassing
edited by Paul De Bruyne & Pascal Gielen
Arts *in* Society
Amsterdam: Valiz, 2011 (2nd ed.: 2013),
ISBN 978-90-78088-50-9

Antennae N° 6
See it Again, Say it Again
The Artist as Researcher
edited by Janneke Wesseling
Amsterdam: Valiz, 2011, ISBN 978-90-78088-53-0

Antennae N° 7
Teaching Art in the Neoliberal Realm
Realism versus Cynicism
edited by Pascal Gielen & Paul De Bruyne
Arts *in* Society
Amsterdam: Valiz, 2012
(2nd ed.: 2013),
ISBN 978-90-78088-57-8

Antennae N° 8
Institutional Attitudes
Instituting Art in a Flat World
edited by Pascal Gielen
Arts *in* Society
Amsterdam: Valiz, 2013, ISBN 978-90-78088-68-4

Antennae N° 9
Dread
The Dizziness of Freedom
edited by Juha van 't Zelfde
Amsterdam: Valiz, 2013, ISBN 978-90-78088-81-3

Antennae N° 10
Participation Is Risky
Approaches to Joint Creative Processes
edited by Liesbeth Huybrechts
Amsterdam: Valiz, 2014, ISBN 978-90-78088-77-6

Antennae N° 11
The Ethics of Art
Ecological Turns in the Performing Arts
edited by Guy Cools & Pascal Gielen
Arts *in* Society
Amsterdam: Valiz, 2014, ISBN 978-90-78088-87-5

Antennae N° 12
Alternative Mainstream
Making Choices in Pop Music
Gert Keunen (author)
Arts *in* Society
Amsterdam: Valiz, 2014,
ISBN 978-90-78088-95-0

Antennae N° 13
The Murmuring of the Artistic
Global Art, Politics and Post-Fordism
Pascal Gielen (author)
Completely revised and enlarged edition of Antennae N° 3
Arts *in* Society
Amsterdam: Valiz, 2015,
ISBN 978-94-92095-04-6

Antennae N° 14
Aesthetic Justice
Intersecting Artistic and Moral Perspectives
edited by Pascal Gielen &
Niels Van Tomme
Arts *in* Society
Amsterdam: Valiz, 2015,
ISBN 978-90-78088-86-8

Antennae N° 15
No Culture, No Europe
On the Foundation of Politics
edited by Pascal Gielen
Arts *in* Society
Amsterdam: Valiz, 2015,
ISBN 978-94-92095-03-9

Antennae N° 16
Arts Education Beyond Art
Teaching Art in Times of Change
edited by Barend van Heusden &
Pascal Gielen
Arts *in* Society
Amsterdam: Valiz, 2015,
ISBN 978-90-78088-85-1

Antennae N° 17
Mobile Autonomy
Exercises in Artists' Self-Organization
edited by Nico Dockx & Pascal
Gielen
Arts *in* Society
Amsterdam: Valiz, 2015,
ISBN 978-94-92095-10-7

Antennae N° 18
Moving Together
Theorizing and Making
Contemporary Dance
Rudi Laermans (author)
Arts *in* Society
Amsterdam: Valiz, 2015,
ISBN 978-90-78088-52-3

Antennae N° 19
Spaces for Criticism
Shifts in Contemporary Art Discourses
edited by Thijs Lijster, Suzana
Milevska, Pascal Gielen,
Ruth Sonderegger
Arts *in* Society
Amsterdam: Valiz, 2015,
ISBN 978-90-78088-75-2

Antennae N° 20
Interrupting the City
Artistic Constitutions of the Public Sphere
edited by Sander Bax, Pascal Gielen
& Bram Ieven
Arts *in* Society
Amsterdam: Valiz, 2015,
ISBN 978-94-92095-02-2

Antennae N° 21
In-between Dance Cultures
On the Migratory Artistic Identity of
Sidi Larbi Cherkaoui and Akram Khan
Guy Cools (author)
Arts *in* Society
Amsterdam: Valiz, 2015,
ISBN 978-94-92095-11-4

Antennae N° 22
Imaginative Bodies
Dialogues in Performance Practices
Guy Cools (author)
Arts *in* Society
Amsterdam: Valiz, 2016,
ISBN 978-94-92095-20-6

Antennae N° 23
The Practice of Dramaturgy
Working on Actions in Performance
edited by Konstantina Georgelou,
Efrosini Protopapa,
Danae Theodoridou
Arts *in* Society
Amsterdam: Valiz, 2017,
ISBN: 978-94-92095-18-3

Antennae N° 24
The Art of Civil Action
Political Space and Cultural Dissent
edited by Philipp Dietachmair,
Pascal Gielen
Arts *in* Society
Amsterdam: Valiz, 2017,
ISBN: 978-94-92095-39-8

Antennae N° 25
Commonism
A New Aesthetics of the Real
Nico Dockx & Pascal Gielen
Arts *in* Society
Amsterdam: Valiz, 2018,
ISBN 978-94-92095-47-3

Antennae N° 26
The Future of the New
Artistic Innovation in Times
of Social Acceleration
Thijs Lijster (ed.)
Arts *in* Society
Amsterdam: Valiz, 2018,
ISBN 978-94-92095-58-9

Antennae N° 27
Contemporary Artist Residencies
Reclaiming Time and Space
edited by Taru Elfving, Pascal
Gielen, Irmeli Kokko
Arts *in* Society
Amsterdam: Valiz, 2018,
ISBN 978-94-92095-46-6